P9-AOF-666

AND THE RISEN BREAD

AND THE RISEN BREAD

Selected Poems, 1957–1997

by

DANIEL BERRIGAN

Edited by JOHN DEAR

FORDHAM UNIVERSITY PRESS
NEW YORK • 1998

LC 98–12691
ISBN 0-8232-1821-x (hardcover)
ISBN 0-8232-1822-8 (paperback)

Library of Congress Cataloging-in-Publication Data

Berrigan, Daniel.
And the risen bread : selected poems, 1957–1997 / by Daniel Berrigan ; edited by John Dear.
p. cm.
ISBN 0-8232-1821-X (hardcover). — ISBN 0-8232-1822-8 (paperback)
I. Dear, John, 1959– . II. Title.
PS3503.E734A64 1998
811′.54—dc21 98-12691
CIP

Printed in the United States of America

Grateful acknowledgment is made to the following publishers for permission to reprint the following material:

1. The Continuum Publishing Company, for:
"In Memoriam, Thomas Merton" (©1969)
2. Beacon Press, for:
Trial Poems, by Daniel Berrigan, with art by Thomas Lewis (©1970)
3. HarperCollins, for:
The Discipline of the Mountain (©1979)
The Mission (©1986)
Stations (©1989)
4. Fortkamp/Rose Hill Books, for:
Homage to Gerard Manley Hopkins (©1993)
5. Augsburg Fortress Press, for:
Isaiah (©1996)
6. Orbis Books, for:
Uncommon Prayer (©1998)
7. Doubleday, for:
eight poems from *Selected and New Poems* by Daniel Berrigan. Copyright © 1973 by Daniel Berrigan. Used by permission of Doubleday, a division of Bantam Doubleday Dell Publishing Group, Inc.

two poems from *The Dark Night of Resistance* by Daniel Berrigan. Copyright © 1971 by Daniel Berrigan. Used by permission of Doubleday, a division of Bantum Doubleday Dell Publishing Group, Inc.

one poem from *America Is Hard to Find* by Daniel Berrigan. Copyright © 1972 by Daniel Berrigan. Used by permission of Doubleday, a division of Bantum Doubleday Dell Publishing Group, Inc.

TO THE NEW YORK WEST SIDE JESUIT COMMUNITY

Some stood and stood and stood.
They were taken for dummies
they were taken for fools
they were taken for being taken in.

Some walked and walked and walked.
They walked the earth
they walked the waters
they walked the air.

Why do you stand?
they were asked, and
why do you walk?

Because of the children, they said, and
because of the heart, and
because of the bread

Because
the cause
is the heart's beat
and the children born
and the risen bread.

CONTENTS

INTRODUCTION

Ross Labrie

Recalling her meeting with Daniel Berrigan at the Poetry Center in New York in the late 1950s, the distinguished poet Denise Levertov has observed that she "would never have imagined that the shy, old-style, young Jesuit" would have become the "bold hero" of the nonviolent movement whom she "grew to admire so much."[1] My own memory of Daniel Berrigan, from roughly the same period, is somewhat different. The names of both Daniel Berrigan and Thomas Merton are a part of my memory of Labre House in Montreal, a house that served the poor and was inspired by the Catholic Worker movement. As someone who had been influenced by theologians like Karl Rahner, Berrigan, who spoke at Labre House on occasion, already then had an acute sense of the church's necessary involvement in the world and its needs. Berrigan presented the Christian God as the "God of history," a God not only concerned with history but "within history." The consequence of this, Berrigan argued, was that the Christian's witness was both "on behalf of history, and beckoned beyond it."[2] Because of this attitude to history the early and late Daniel Berrigans seem to me to be quite continuous with each other.

As a Jesuit seminarian Berrigan bristled under the abstractness that marked his numerous years of study, referring to the years spent studying philosophy in particular as the "driest dust ever to settle around the spirit of the ages."[3] Nevertheless, Berrigan's devotion to the Jesuit way of life has been lifelong, even if not always reciprocated by those of his fellow Jesuits who disapproved of his acts of civil disobedience. Recalling his entry as a young man into the Jesuit novitiate in 1939, Berrigan has said

---

[1] Denise Levertov, "Living What You Believe," *Apostle of Peace: Essays in Honor of Daniel Berrigan*, ed. John Dear (Maryknoll, N.Y.: Orbis, 1996), p. 103.

[2] Daniel Berrigan,. *Consequences: Truth And . . .* (New York: Macmillan, 1967), p. 29.

[3] Daniel Berrigan, *To Dwell in Peace* (San Francisco: Harper & Row, 1987), p. 101.

that he "fell in love immediately and incurably with the Jesuit style."[4] In Berrigan's eyes the Jesuit paradigm provided the church with individuals whose responsibility it was to know not only their religion but also the world—so as to "undergo its terrifying crises, to stand at the side of perplexed and hard-pressed" human beings.[5]

Among the many people who inspired Berrigan's development as a priest, social activist, and poet there were three in particular who were especially significant. One of these was Dorothy Day, the founder of the Catholic Worker movement. When Daniel Berrigan was growing up on the family farm just outside of Syracuse, New York, Dorothy Day's penny-a-copy newspaper, the *Catholic Worker,* was always around the house. When Berrigan taught at LeMoyne College in the 1950s, Day would come as a guest to speak to Berrigan's student protegés, who were being awakened to the need for social reform both in Syracuse and in the Third World. Along with Peter Maurin, Dorothy Day, sometimes defiantly, had awakened the social consciousness of an American church that had just begun to adjust to respectability within the American mainstream. Virtually ignored by the Catholic hierarchy in the 1930s and 1940s, Day urged the church to consider its roots and remember its first mission of service to the poor and oppressed. In Berrigan's view, Dorothy Day, a pacifist, brought a fresh, re-imagined perception of the church to an institution that had been, in Berrigan's words, "stalemated by two centuries of business as usual," having come to take "poverty and war for granted, rhetoric to the contrary notwithstanding." While remaining loyal to the church as the bride of Christ, Day, according to Berrigan, declared "peace, as others declared war."[6] Furthermore, recalling her adamantine spirit, which at times gave rise to social protest, Berrigan has observed that Day always insisted that there was "no mercy without justice."[7]

Thomas Merton was another important influence on Berrigan. The two began a correspondence in the late 1940s, but it was the 1960s before their relationship developed, spurred by the appearance of an article by Merton entitled "The Root of War," which appeared in the *Catholic Worker* in 1961. The article eventually led to Berrigan's participation in an interdenominational retreat given by Merton at his abbey

[4] Daniel Berrigan, *No Bars to Manhood* (Garden City, N.Y.: Doubleday, 1970), p. 12.
[5] Daniel Berrigan, *They Call Us Dead Men* (New York: Macmillan, 1966), p. 169.
[6] Berrigan, *To Dwell*, p. 69.
[7] Daniel Berrigan, *Portraits: Of Those I Love* (New York: Crossroad, 1982), p. 74.

in Gethsemani, Kentucky. From then on, the relationship and friendship grew steadily until Berrigan's involvement in the Catonsville, Maryland draft card burning, at which point Merton, shortly before his accidental death in Thailand in 1968, distanced himself because of his disapproval of civil acts of disobedience which contained even a hint of violence, no matter how closely related to the cause of peace. In a circular letter to friends Merton had come around somewhat in the summer of 1968, writing that his "good friends" Daniel and Philip Berrigan "believe that as Christians they must protest against a futile and immoral war to the point where they are jailed for protest."[8] As the correspondence between Merton and Berrigan reveals, the two men, coming from quite different parts of the church, taught each other through the 1960s an approach to social issues that rested upon the complementarity of contemplation and action. Thus, Merton the monk wrote in a spirit of protest about social ills like the Vietnam War and racism while Berrigan, increasingly involved in frontline protest, immersed himself in religious texts and in liturgy prior to conducting protest action.

Daniel Berrigan was drawn into the Catonsville protest, which eventually led to his serving an eighteen-month sentence in a federal penitentiary, by his brother, Philip, who visited him at Cornell, in 1968, where Daniel was the Associate Director of an experimental, interdenominational program called United Religious Work. Daniel's admiration for and loyalty to Philip has never wavered, and he has recalled Philip's example as an emboldening one, drawing "less hardy spirits such as myself."[9] If Merton drew Berrigan toward the contemplative dimension of social protest, Philip drew him toward the white heat of nonviolent confrontation.

Rather like Merton, Berrigan has been as committed to writing, especially the writing of poetry, as to the life of social activism. The two sides of Berrigan's life have always been intertwined, but particularly so since the 1960s, when the life of social activism became the subject of the poetry and the poetry in turn created an aesthetic lens by which Berrigan distilled and thereby set into intellectual and spiritual perspective the essential lessons of his life as an activist. In addition, the poetry placed Berrigan in another space in which he could, even fleetingly, withdraw

[8] Thomas Merton, *The Road to Joy: The Letters of Thomas Merton to Old and New Friends,* ed. Robert Daggy (New York: Farrar Straus & Giroux, 1989), p. 116.

[9] Berrigan, *To Dwell*, p. 199.

from the demands of the activist life, allowing him to nourish other interests and other tastes. In particular, the poetry brought him into contact with the beautiful and the holy, which in turn enhanced the value of that divinely created life which he was struggling to protect in the social and political arena.

Berrigan's father had written a good deal of verse, much of it force-fed to his sons who thereby became more alienated from poetry than would otherwise have been the case. While Berrigan did not respect his father's poetry, he was affected by his father's reading of it—the sounds and rhythms of it. His father, though, had no sympathy for modern poetry, which Berrigan only came to discover during his years in Jesuit training. In those years, he has said, he came to know the poetry of Hopkins and Eliot, Frost and Pound—as well as others who had "formed the sensibility of his generation."[10] As compared with Hopkins, for whom religion was primarily a source of beauty, for Berrigan it was a preeminently a source of knowledge about reality. In an essay on sacred art in *They Call Us Dead Men* (1966) he wrote that Christian art had the great advantage of being in the "real world," of having "grasped things as they are."[11] It was a short step from such a view to a perception of the role of poetry as illuminating contemporary culture as nothing else could—like an "all-night nurse," Berrigan added pithily, at the bedside of a "dying patient."[12]

Berrigan's interest in art was flanked by his interest in the imagination in drawing human beings to a full sense of their dignity and of the moral choices open to them. In *The Bow in the Clouds* (1961) he emphasized that the imagination "defines the Christian, and it frees him."[13] For Berrigan the great symbols of Judeo-Christian culture engaged the imagination, not forcing a response, but drawing the Christian toward an application of those symbols to his or her own time. In this way the Christian's response to the world would be ever fresh and renewed.

Berrigan's commitment to the imagination was never so high as in his first volume, *Time Without Number* (1957), which was nominated for a National Book Award and given the prestigious Lamont Prize for Poetry

[10] Ibid., p. 96.

[11] Daniel Berrigan, "Sacred Art and the Life of Man," *They Call Us Dead Men* (New York: Macmillan, 1966), p. 101.

[12] Berrigan, *Portraits*, p. 27.

[13] Daniel Berrigan, *The Bow in the Clouds: Man's Covenant With God* (New York: Coward-McCann, 1961), p. 67.

by the American Academy of Arts and Letters. The book was published by Macmillan on the advice of Marianne Moore, who on the book's dust jacket characterized the poems as "revealed" as well as "written." The book, which went into three printings, reflected Berrigan's life during the 1950s—notably his sabbatical in France, including his meeting with the worker priests, who were suppressed by Rome shortly thereafter. Without in any way compromising his allegiance to the priesthood and to the Jesuits, the year in France allowed Berrigan to feel the freedom of himself as a human being—as he recalled some years later.[14]

While some of the conceptualizing and phrasing in *Time Without Number* is conventional, as in the line "These are the nettles sprung from sweating Cain" in the poem, "The Workers," nevertheless most of the language is original and telling, as in these lines from "Exaltavit Humiles:"

> Sumac jostled
> by shouldering oaks to the forest edge—how it burns
> clearer than they. And cobweb, no more than an afterthought,
> trembles at dawn like new-hammered silver.
> The crouching rocks; overlaid
> with purest lace. . . .
> Roots, bound hand and foot, hear and heave mightily,
> lie cruciform, await the breaking spell.

Structurally, these filigreed lines are impressive. The cobweb motif breathlessly not only gathers the blood-red sumac and tree roots, but evolves itself into the figure of the crucifix with its transcendental power of straddling the natural and the supernatural. Furthermore, the inclusion of roots and rocks in the overall design extends the poem's geography so that the humblest aspects of being are turned toward God.

Many of the poems with their images of birches and stones remind one of Frost's poetry. While Frost's birches and stones convey an upward sweep that carries the reader toward a momentary stay against confusion, as Frost put it, Berrigan's are as likely to symbolize a swelling of the ground that gets history moving. such is in these lines in "Lightning Struck Here:"

---

[14] Daniel Berrigan, *No Bars to Manhood* (Garden City, N.Y.: Doubleday, 1970), pp. 13–14.

> If stones can dream, after some hundred years
> shouldering weight, making a wall inch onward
> heaving it up a hill, braking its roll . . .
> if stones can long to stand up naked, a new creation
> a horizon. . . .
> I suppose the dream
> might rise, might arc, take color and stance of these
> birches that fan out suddenly, bursting the wall
> so when we come on them, all that remains
> is a shambles. Lightning struck here
> is a first thought. But no: a dream
> shook from the mud, the interminable years, and lives.

Thus, if Berrigan is all too aware of the descending God in his poetry, he is equally aware of the upwelling of human beings. In part this reflects Berrigan's sense of the rising of human beings spiritually from their lethargy as fallen creatures. In part, though, it reflects Berrigan's American egalitarianism, always a part of his Catholicism, in which history rises, as Thoreau and Whitman had called for, from the awakened consciousnesses of ordinary people.

The reconciliation of the absoluteness implicit in Berrigan's vision as a Catholic and his ingrained skepticism as a Jeffersonian American gave rise eventually to a fundamental tension about authority, as can be seen in his wry poem, "O Catholic Church," published in the later volume, *May All Creatures Live*. In that poem Berrigan urges the church to speak with authority ("a forefinger pointing—a voice saying 'north' "), but the plea is hedged by the reference to Pope John XXIII, whose authority was reflected in the all but unanimous assent of the Catholic church. In the period following the death of this pope Berrigan categorizes the church as having been weakened by "bickering, meandering, not knowing / *Do not* from doughnut, north from south." One of the things that makes Berrigan interesting as a writer is the tension between his consciousness of the heroic dimensions of his faith and his sometimes angry consciousness of his church's failure as an institution.

Drawn in the 1950s to the historical consciousness of theologians such as Jean Danielou and Karl Rahner, Berrigan felt himself drawn back to early Christianity and especially to the charismatic Christ of the Gospels who, Berrigan believed, had sometimes been obscured beneath the emphasis of the Catholic church on dogmatic theology and Thomist philosophy since the Council of Trent. In *Consequences: Truth And . . .* Berrigan wrote that the time had come to recall what was "seen as essential by the first Christians" in an effort to touch the "springs of our being."[15] In a related statement, included in an essay on sacred art in *They Call Us Dead Men*, Berrigan described the Christ of the early Christians as "adult" and "victorious."[16] In a sense Berrigan's emphasis upon early Christianity was an implicit challenge to the more recent institutional history of the church, but Berrigan's divided perception of the early and later church tended to remain emotionally contained in the poetry of the 1950s. Typical of that period is the exquisite poem, "Each day Writes:"

> Christ, to whose eyes flew,
> whose human heart knew, or furious or slow,
> the dark wingbeat of time: your presence give
> light to my eyeless mind, reason to my heart's rhyme.

Apart from the sophisticated play on the motifs of darkness and light, blindness and sight, together with the trenchant linking of art and life which are both marked by a wingbeat or rhythm, one admires the chiseled precision of the poem's diction and its evocative patterning of sound. There is the skillful use of internal rhyming, for example, in the assonant uniting of the terms of the last two lines through the pervasive distribution of the long "i" sound.

In 1963 Berrigan spent a sabbatical year abroad, initially in Paris, then in eastern Europe, finally in South Africa. The traveling, which included an interdenominational peace conference in Prague, opened his eyes to the way in which his own country was viewed from outside, particularly with respect to its involvement in the Vietnam War. On his return to the United States Berrigan became actively involved in the public protest of the war and in the struggle for racial integration. One of the results of his protest activity was to incur the wrath of Cardinal Spellman, the ordinary of the diocese where Berrigan lived. Spellman, whose public support for the military was well-known, saw to it that Berrigan was sent on an open-ended journalistic mission to Latin America, an experience that, with its glimpses of unendurable poverty and official corrup-

[15] Berrigan, *Consequences*, p. 10.
[16] Berrigan, *They Call Us Dead Men*, p. 93.

tion, radicalized Berrigan. He had left the leafy surroundings of the academy behind him.

In the 1960s Berrigan's poetry gradually became more and more associated with his own experience and thus less directed toward biblical subjects and general spiritual themes. Increasingly, the poems centered on issues of conscience and the emotional atmosphere of the poetry became more volatile. Moreover, Berrigan's poetic diction became somewhat less traditional as he attempted to register the horrors of war. An example is the poem, "A Pittsburgh Beggar Reminds Me of the Dead of Hiroshima" in *No One Walks Waters* (1966). Looking up at a "Greek sky / where five stars make a god," a nostalgic view of an orderly universe, Berrigan is reminded instead of a sky that had rained down nuclear death:

> I am too unschooled to know,
> befouled and blinded by the hot droppings
> that struck my eyes in sleep, from the great bird
> the descending fecal horror.
> I stood and shook like ague
> —Hiroshima, Nagasaki—
> the ungentle names of my memory's youth,
> the blue remembered hills
> tipping like hell's buckets all their
> hot afterbirth on me.

The poem's images of the "fecal horror" and "hot afterbirths" dispensed by the bombers communicate the savagery of war not only in a moral sense but through language that bluntly conveys a palpable revulsion against war.

In the 1960s Berrigan became more alienated than ever from the scholarly approach to war within the official church, a view which he perceived in the teaching style of some of his own Jesuit colleagues. An example is "His Cleric's Eye" in *No One Walks Waters*," which focuses on a priest who died at forty. The poem is anything but elegiac, though:

> His mind was lucid, ingrained. He would say,
> *it is deductibly verified*
> *that God is immutable; and,*
> *universal order converges on one being.*

While the italicized lines reproduce the bookish dryness of the dead priest's voice and hence the poem's theme of the wasted life, the poem's moral strength lies in Berrigan's hope that the eyes of the priest will be opened in the presence of Christ, who will "stitch you through the needle's eye, the grudging gate" following the priest's belated passage through the "crotch of being." This latter image again conveys something of the startling bluntness of some of Berrigan's poetic phrasing in the 1960s and 1970s, a feature of the Beat poetry with whose iconoclastic stance he had to some extent identified.

The year 1968 was an intense one for Berrigan. He flew to Hanoi representing the peace movement in order to be present at the release of three American fliers; he joined his brother, Philip, in a draft card burning incident in Catonsville, Maryland that resulted in both their imprisonments; and he had to bear the sudden, accidental death of Thomas Merton in Thailand. Subsequent to the Catonsville trial Berrigan would spend some months as a fugitive from the law, a period of his life that has been described in an electrifying volume of prose-poetry entitled *The Dark Night of Resistance* (1971). As a convicted felon—even if one associated with the non-violent resistance movement—Berrigan raised eyebrows within his church, his order, and even within his own family. In the poem, "False Gods, Real Men," the title poem of a volume brought out in 1969, Berrigan reflected sadly upon the wound to his family's pride, a family that had produced two sons who had become priests and which had sent four sons to fight for their country. In this regard Berrigan wrote in *No Bars to Manhood* (1970) that at Catonsville he and his fellow anti-war activists had "attacked an underlying, optimistic, unassailably stubborn proposition: that the American instance is in fact a good example of the way civilized men conduct themselves."[17] While Berrigan has always been passionately American, his perception in the late 1960s was that the United States had fallen drastically from its high ideological traditions.

My brother and I stand like the fences
    of abandoned farms, changed times
    too loosely webbed against
        deicide homicide
A really powerful blow
    would bring us down like scarecrows.

[17] Berrigan, *No Bars to Manhood*, p. 50.

Nature, knowing this, finding us mildly useful
    indulging also
    her backhanded love of freakishness
        allows us to stand.

Not only does the subject matter of the poem suggest a voice situated at the outskirts of society, but the form mirrors this position as well with its shard-like images and raggedly unevenness lines, a reflection of Berrigan's bold forays into free verse at the time.

Also typical of this period is the mordant poem about Berrigan's eighteen-month incarceration in Danbury penitentiary, "Almost Everybody Is Dying Here: Only a Few Actually Make It." The poem, which appeared in *Prison Poems* (1973), was intended to express the torment of all of the prisoners at Danbury who, in their longing for death, witness to the effect of society's treatment of them. In the poem Berrigan emblematically records the death of a man whose head suddenly fell to one side "as though to underscore some unassuageable grief." The indirectness and irony of the words "as though" are overwhelming and, in a sense, unanswerable following the man's death, but they also express the wit that continued to flicker inside the embattled poet. The survival of this wit, by which I mean the play of mind over experience, is remarkable, given the exhausting pace of Berrigan's involvement in social activism during the 1970s.

Elizabeth Bartelme, Berrigan's longtime editor and friend, has noted that Berrigan's voice as a poet modulated from the "lyrical to apocalyptic, from wonder at the beauty of the world to disgust at the ugliness human beings have made of it."[18] There would seem to be truth in this observation if one looks at the poems of the 1970s and early 1980s. Representative of this aspect of Berrigan's writing are a number of rapidly written, fluidly structured, and uncompromisingly prophetic volumes such as *A Book of Parables* (1977), *Uncommon Prayer* (1978), *Beside the Sea of Glass* (1978), *The Discipline of the Mountain* (1979), *Ten Commandments for the Long Haul* (1981), and *The Nightmare of God* (1983). While some of these uneven books contained poems, the best poetry of the period was collected in *May All Creatures Live* (1984). There the apocalyptic tone met with artistic resistance in the form of a disciplined

---

[18] Elizabeth Bartelme, "A Poet for Difficult Times," *Apostle of Peace: Essays in Honor of Daniel Berrigan*, edited by John Dear (Maryknoll, N.Y.: Orbis, 1996), p. 108.

approach to poetic phrasing that has characterized Berrigan's finest work. The contents of the poems also exhibit a fruitful tension—as in the poem, "Fidelity," which is about a picture framer who, in the midst of New York's toxic urban decay, remains shiningly faithful to his dying wife:

> On this foul foot path,
> mule track, death mile, oblivion alley, bloody pass
> Broadway, pith and paradigm of the world, cutting the
> 50 states of Amnesia like a poisoned pie; a swollen Styx
> an Augean drain ditch
> a lotus blooms.

Moving rapidly through the onrushing lines, which capture the city's mad pace and the sardonically-seen cultural symbol of Broadway, the reader is suddenly arrested by the initially inexplicable image of the lotus, Berrigan's tribute to the picture framer.

The poetry written after the mid-1980s, including the radiant poems from *Block Island* (1985) and *Homage to Gerard Manley Hopkins* (1993), marks a return to calmer waters. Here is an example from Berrigan's tribute to Hopkins:

> Such sweetness overtakes
> for thought of you, whose thought
> like a sleeping child
> on banked violets
> waking, sees all around
> for what it saw
> a sweetness more intense.

In addition to the evocativeness and tenderness of feeling, one notices how words like "thought" and "sweetness" turn back upon themselves and are of obvious interest to the poet as language—as distinct from his theme.

It has been over twenty years since Berrigan's poems were collected in a volume that has been long out of print. The poems in this new collection, which incorporates minor revisions by the author, bring the reader of Berrigan's poetry up to date and are thus welcome. The publication of these poems allows Berrigan's poetry to be seen by readers who may not have seen it before, either because they belong to a new generation of readers or perhaps because when many of the poems were written Berrigan's life far overshadowed his poetry and was thus a prior subject of interest. In this connection one is reminded of Thoreau's famous remark that he could not both live his life and utter it. As with Thoreau, however, Berrigan has managed, to a remarkable extent, to do both. It is hoped that the present volume will stimulate critical interest in a contemporary American poet who has related some significant social and political history and who has shown the power of art to transform the ordeal of social protest into the sorts of precise articulations in which the mind can find solace.

1. Time Without Number

CREDENTIALS

I would it were possible to state in so
few words my errand in the world: quite simply
forestalling all inquiry, the oak offers his leaves
largehandedly. And in winter his integral magnificent order
decrees, says solemnly who he is
in the great thrusting limbs that are all finally
one: a return, a permanent riverandsea.

So the rose is its own credential, a certain
unattainable effortless form: wearing its heart
visibly, it gives us heart too: bud, fulness and fall.

EACH DAY WRITES

                                        in my heart's core
ineradicably, what it is to be man.

Hours and hours, no sun rises, night sits
kenneled in me: or spring, spring's
flowering seizes me in an hour.

I tread my heart amazed: what land,
what skies are these, whose shifting weathers
now shrink my harvest to a stack of bones;
now weigh my life with glory?

                                        Christ, to whose eyes flew,
whose human heart knew, or furious or slow,
the dark wingbeat of time: your presence give
light to my eyeless mind, reason to my heart's rhyme.

STARS ALMOST ESCAPE US

                                                    They come unwilling
to greatness, unlike dramatic trees

in chorus, miming destiny
with want and plenty, with grinning or tragic
masks.

Size makes no difference. Nor have stars taken
easily to being something other. Their blossoming
momentarily in hedges, depends on
stillness: let him come near, and the doe's eye leaps,
the fireflies leap into a thicket or heaven.

You may decline a whole night of stars
by lighting or snuffing a candle in a closet.
Not one, or all their sum of light taken together,
can keep a stranger's feet on his tricky road.

For what then?
the true, the beautiful struggles
in winds and spaces, and scarcely, perilously wins

I AM RENEWED

to rising by that sun
sets courage like a summer round my roots
and welcomes me to stature.

I am renewed to breathing by that bread
sent like a sunrise to my dark
bringing me someday morrow.

My blood that walks as sullen as a millstream
trumpets the joining of that wine of His.

My life that folds to burial grows bold
and hobbled in its windings climbs the grave.

My ashen words puff up in flame
infused with four winds of a word *arise*.

My hollow breast takes heart at hearing Him
sing like a star above its broken roof.

My feet clear gardens in the greying snow:
my winters die for mention of His name.

O let these words remind His wounds of me

BIRTHDAY IN QUEBEC

(eighty-six)

I

I remember today a roadside, the crucifix
raised crude as life among farming people,
its shadow creeping, dawn and twilight, over their lives.
Among wains, haycocks and men it moved like a savior.

So old, so scored by their winters, it had been staked out
perhaps by a band of ruffians on first Good Friday.
The way it endured, time would have bruised his fist in striking it.

What time had done, breaking the bones at knee and wrist,
washing the features blank as quarry stone,
turning the legs to spindles, stealing the eyes

was only to plant forever its one great gesture
deeper in furrow, heave it high above rooftops.

Where time had done his clumsy worst, cracking its heart,
hollowing its breast inexorably,—he opened this Burning-glass
to hold the huge landscape: crops, houses and men, in Its fire.

II

He was irremovably there, nailing down the landscape,
more permanent than any mountain time could bring down
or frost alter face of. He could not be turned aside
from his profound millennial prayer: not by birds

moved wonderfully to song on that cruel bough:
not by sun, standing compassionately at right hand or left.

Let weathers tighten or loosen his nails: he was vowed to stand.
Northstar took rise from his eyes, learned constancy of him.
Let cloudburst break like judgment, sending workmen homeward
whipping their teams from field, down the rutted road to barn

still his body took punshment like a mainsail
bearing the heaving world onward to the Father.

And we knew nightlong: in the clear morning he will be there,
not to be pulled down from landscape, never from his people's
        hearts.

EVERYTHING THAT IS

                                        is not something other:
a ridiculous pablum for the poet's mind
until the wind sing it, or star bring it
ringing its name through the astonished night:

or on a March day, the crocus
struggle into air.
                                        Or the autumn maple *glory! glory!*
puzzle the strollers with its identical form
four months later assumed again.
                                        Such things shake the mind
backward, inward:
                                I wonder who knew the stars
from flowers, before flowers were not stars:
before trees spread
                                between one and other
                    a growth
by night starlike, by day a flowering?

ITS PERFECT HEART

It was November: an invisible fire
freshened the heart of the grey-blue heron
that had drifted and loved contented
on mild streams, among summer dwellings and children.

But what aroused it powerfully
that it shook earth like a disease, pettiness and location,
to set breast against wearying universal air?

Now while dawn streams upward from fields
or early stars send us to fireside
still it labors above by day and night
starting the sunrise, shadowing the red leaning moon;

sufficient, remote from longing
as we look aloft: vowed to greatness
and powerfully steered by its lodestone, its perfect heart.

THE MOON

This desolate cold god
never created a flower
in his salty furrow,
or called noble birds to climb
and drink at his vein of fire:

he never walked the noon
alight with his own light
whose trees were his sudden fountains
whose waterfalls stood and shouted:

but shod and ribbed in ice
he keeps heart averted
from the plague of youth, from growth:

he has sworn his cold eye
never will heat or approve
the blood that rounds our breast
and grows the fruit hung there:

poet, mystic, lover
claim his glance for their own:
but only the dead who never
lift eye or cry, or name him
shall own him at the end:

since he and they dwell far
above, below mobbing desire,
and indifferent to each other
separate go their way
into no human day.

THE WORKERS

This is the body the seasons sold for money—
one by one they guarded and grew his frame:
we were hardly ready for him and he was ready.
This is the one.

These are the nettles sprung from sweating Cain.
Gather them up: they are holier far than flowers:
let us see the brow of the laborer glisten with them.
These are the thorns.

These are the coldiron embers of Lucifer:
these are the arrogant stars pushed out of heaven.
Then give him a handful of stars: heap stars at his feet.
These are the nails.

This is the prime redwood of all the world.
It is tougher and taller than he: it will swing him high:
it will hold him high forever if so we wish.
This is the cross.

HERE THE STEM RISES

deflowered forever.

the bird is wise only
in ways of quiet

time is a lithe fruit
bending above us

too old for comfort
too raw for falling

here no slim morning
steps out of the sea

no season of snow
no hear-ye of thunder

no chameleon crawling
of youth or of age

not even a now
nor an I nor a you

how many the folded
hands. O how lovely

the words never spoken

EXALTAVIT HUMILES

All things despised, capricious, cranky,
have an hour of morning. Sumac jostled
by shouldering oaks to the forest edge—how it burns
clearer than they. And cobweb, no more than an afterthought,
trembles at dawn like new-hammered silver.

The crouching rocks; overlaid
with purest lace.

The wild brown grasses;
a canticle at the furnace door:
Bless the Lord, rime at morning, frost and cold air!

Roots, bound hand and foot, hear and heave mightily,
lie cruciform, await the breaking spell.

For a moment nothing is wasted, nothing of no moment:
to the banquet grace calls, grace clothes the unwanted poor.

I SING

the star whose light
my song makes steady,
the face whose look was never
but when my hand had found it,
the word that lovelier stayed
than trees unstressed by season,
what on the earth was seldom
less seldom for my speaking—
pride, delight, deliverance.

This is not greatness, no:
not that consummate gesture
from king whose *fiat fiat*
is blue on distance blue.
His tree-end never dragged
across my coward foothill:
his manacles and thorns
have never clawed or kinged me.

Not these. But few and lonely
the unregarded wait me
to say their *beautiful*
with breath and heart I borrowed:

who but for self I lent
would like me fret and clutter
and be themselves for never.

LIGHTNING STRUCK HERE

If stones can dream, after some hundred years
shouldering weight, making a wall inch onward
heaving it up a hill, braking its roll,
being only half above ground, taking the crack

of frost, the infernal sun, the insinuating, sleepy moss:—
if stones can long to stand up naked, a new creation
a horizon; where the wall goes
what shires, forests, it holds—
I suppose the dream
might rise, might arc, take color and stance of these
birches that fan out suddenly, bursting the wall
so when we come on them, all that remains
is a shambles. Lightning struck here
is a first thought. But no: a dream
shook from the mud, the interminable years, and lives

THE GOSPEL ACCORDING TO ME

1. LONELINESS (Joseph speaks)

To be a part of things, to be apart from them:

Every spring I dunged and pruned the peach row
on south hillside: every autumn, like a stranger
took down the fruit whose face met my surprise
with its odor and wet, only half remembered or deserved.

Or watched from a doorway, artisans
summoning out of a dumb stick some form of beauty,
the fine grain emerging along hand or arm like a pulse,
every sigh of the blade saying, *I did not do that.*

Or parleyed with old trees
that shift painfully in the noon wind, heads together
nodding a memory awake. I did not lead them there:
they were already old when my father slept
a boy's drowsy noon in their shade.

I had even less to do with the stars
that having led her to me, bring her still face to me
evening and dawn, making of evening and dawn
one tranquil ecstasy.
                                        Blade, hoe, manhood—
what have my tools to do with What wakes in her?

2. SAID GOD

I would give my Son to them.
In a field of flowers, wide dawn to dusk,
one hesitant flower more, only one more:

in a sky already great with stars,
one star more at the edge, hardly in evening.

He will not make turmoil: one child more
led by his father's hand into a park of children:
one voice adds little: one voice to a choir,
another among the swings, linked in a ring-around.

They take him easily to heart: more is but
merrier: he asks
so little of heart or world. He will never trouble
the country children of men with who am I

Only to pause intent over their games. Never to say
Children: I am all your bloom and odor and starlight.

3. THE COAT

This is the coat His mother fitted
at hearthlight weeping fondly. In three seasons—
summer was her angel, fall bent her boughs

crone winter mothered her maidenhead—
she stitched Him in and out by the nodding fire:
O heartbeat soft as snow on high snow falling,
vein as the veined grape delicate,
my body's shuttle closes you in white linen.

This is the coat my mother's love went buying
to warm me, naked and shivering one
she heard all night peeking her heart for shelter.
This skin she buttoned to my chin, these eyes
she kissed to light, and gave me over
to the stinging hand of twelvemonth winter.

It wears me well. She in cunning stole me
from the bolt Christ, won my pattern
wheedling and whispering with Mary at a churchdoor.
I am more kin of Him than hers
who cut and seamed me till her body bled.

O see Him live in me, not I:
I put him on and strut my coat-of-pie.

4. IN SUM, LIKE THIS

Who you are
let astounded midnight say
that saw itself flooded with day

or springtime that came around
subtly on the world's wheel
and saw you, small and larger, walking its ground

or suave on a boy's tongue
the air making your words
and taking them grandly, a whole summer of birds:

let that mother tell
whose earth and heaven were small
between hearthside and village well

or the dumb tree that bears
pegged down, posted as ours
forever, the unsearchable human years.

5. THE MEN ON THE HILL

There is still time to escape
the hill where ruin hangs,
the dry, lax throat of doom.

Tall as veiled spears they hem him,
the proud and diehard women.
Their hearts bleed in their eyes,
their eyes run on to death, their wits
in little feeble rivers run the ground.

Mark what holds them still:—
his spastic dying cry:
for murderers no 1ightning:
a thirst to curse all springs
our tongues are laid against.

There is less than nothing here.
Nothing were yet something
if stones would rise and grate
a syllable of God: if hands were sprung
a moment only from the trap of nails.

But death has staked him off
and bound him for its baggage:
heaving no miracle, the hill
sighs to a long sun westward:

the sky runs red with torches,
the city blinks us blind
and only death is savior.

6. PLAY SAFE; His Friends

Of course death was hard, hard for the poor.
Yet one finally took it in stride,
closing a father's eyes, seeing the mild slumbering
seas turn monstrous.

But this:

God, unutterable,
friend, mildly poured
over days and years. What words were left us
(this hard exchange, this other side of death?)

Whether we turned locks in a remote alley
or pushed off into seas and stars: the dawn
rose to him, evening breathed him
It was always
never again to be safe, summed up our lives.

7. BELIEVE

That delicate honeycomb Christ took to mouth,
that plundered nest was sweet, to lips grown grey
with Judas kiss and gall. Not since Mary's milk
had earth offered in cup or lip
such words as bees, this way and that shifting
assuring: the dead flower lives: even death serves.

The dismembered fish too,
ikthus for Christ, stared up at the fearful
fishermen. They tossed unseaworthy
when the walker of waves stood there; the floor
pitched them green. When he had eaten away all
but literal arrangement, the skeleton said with its mouth
Jesus Christ, Son of God, Savior.
Death again: the eyes
even of a dead fish crying: *believe or drown.*

8. GOOD NEWS IN A BAD TIME

Women who come to mummy you: trees
on that road, stood in commencing flesh
and said with a new tongue

I am risen. A hundred resurrections lined the dawn
but they thought: we will give his ghost cold comfort

and wind him like a Pharaoh in long linen.
They had nothing to offer life. Of what use in that mouth

honeycomb or fish? He must grow his own flesh
a tree from its root.

They stand where he cast the squared stone aside.
They run and run, but the news

is far as the tremendous drowning
world of trees, that drank from his infinite
roots: runs far ahead, far as years
as morning, as this unhurried tree.

9. THE BIG WIND

Their lives rounded in a backcountry brogue
now to see, at crowd's edge, the fine Athenian profiles
agape, scenting their delicate language like
odor of muscatel or honey:

Peter and John, it is Babel crashing about your ears.
The Spirit, impatient of gross and exquisite tongues, of known
and unknown gods, has riven the abominable tower
The undivided tongues

are abroad, are a wildfire,

You; never again constrained
by scarecrow gestures, by hem or haw. You; to see
agonized at the crowd's edge, tbe faces emptied of guile,
their human wisdom consumed in a stench of straw.

LITTLE HOURS

I

Mother, at that word your eloquent body spoke
I search another word vainly as Gabriel.

O witnessing your consent, he saw
an axis planted deep in our human soil;
history, fear, defeat, aeons and nations
turned, would turn forever about your village room
declaring like figures in time's rickety tower
the lightning strike, this only and central hour.

Whom the world could not contain is detained in you.

Since Love in entering, so builds your hidden doorway,
consent again, receive me for child I pray:
your nourishment, your silence, your face averted,
your hands serving excellent bread and meat: your heart
apart in its own country, heaven descended
to four low walls and a dim evening fire.

II

Winter is hard: it reminds us how that mother,
heavy and meek at term, set foot on her dolorous road.
Her trees, ample and tender at summer
were slit and groaning beggars the wind went through:
the sun that clothed and companied her angel:
what fierce looks from him, and scant comfort now!

Mother: because the ungracious season did not rise
—at your footfall, for knowledge of whom you carried,—
leap cliffs with roses, melt the tigerlike ice
into tame brooks for you—

because north wind blew
and summer hid—enter stilly my heart
whose winter your footfall breaks all apart.

III

Like a waterfall, from what height falling
he came to her; falling, filling her body.
That vessel brimming with him, O never shall fail.

or entered her like a sun its morning, starting what flowers—
from her footfall and welcome, an inextinguishable day.
that dawn lifting light to us, O never shall darkness own.

or came in echoes of that living anvil
forming him, calling him: be loud in me, love O loud:
until his thunders owned her breast utterly.

he came as tongue to her bells. O from that shaken
and living tower, what music flies: my soul
does magnify who makes my body great.

or came in a tide, riding her pure lands under—
tender, O living rain: he fell to her to rise
in hundredfolds up from her secret garden.

But mostly in need, asking her flesh to clothe him.
O because love ran uncontrollably to that meeting,
from her arms, her breast, He walks into our lives.

2. Encounters

EVE

It was for love of me
Adam undid Christ. And I must encounter
of my sour body that golden fruit
Mary; and say to her

how firm we wove and grasped
the ropes that scourged him
what thorns we grew, our first tears'
harvest for his crown.

Woman to woman's heart
I will go. Miles are years from Eden to that hill
but I will take for sign, if so she know me
blood on my face

I will follow
the unhealed scar the tree Christ dragged
opens in time

the poor go
for comfort to the poor.

Across years, across the stilled
hearts of our sons: drawing the vicious
thornbrake aside, sundering the serpentine rope
her hand reaches my own.

ABEL

One blood veined us, stem and fruit
weighing our mother Eve. *Brothers*
said her burning eyes: *see, hand*
must lock in hand: fingers root
in no rock than this other: Abel
in Cain, younger in his brother.

My mother, the worm that raveled Eden
tents in the parent tree.
                                        New lambs
sniff and shy at my blood: go red fleece
teach death to my mother.

ABRAHAM

To see my small son
running ahead: pausing above a flower,
bringing some trifle of hedgerow
wearying, sighing, seeking my hand

unable in all his being
to give death credence,
his heart agile
to prove youth upon a ditch or stile:

to see this you must know
my heart like kettledrums commanded alarms
and marches, shook old age
like treason from its majesty.

My heart now
drums
I am nearer I am death

Who is child now?who is old? my tears
or his song? I am sift of dust
in that Hand unmercifully blown

Love Me, His thunder never cried
Love me
my child's eyes never cried
until this dawn
and under
      under
      my knife

SAINT JOSEPH

She walked noon fields
bearing the child in arms.
Trees stood stock still, even in May wind.

Some task of women
bowed her head, set fingers flying,
a busy stillness at the heart.

Like learning and entering
paradise: from labor to mild joy, from action

to adoration.
At the still center she
and the child aimlessly gathering
wild grasses: into one hand, the scattered leaves gathering
of the universe.

CHRIST

Words are outer form
wherein majesty might near,
if it so please:
of limb and mien not substance,
but light; glancing,
announcing: lo, he cometh.

Words summon her too,
the mother unfolding
like a kerchief, odor and form
of him who lay there:
so in repose her body grew
a spiritual space to round
and radiate you:

friends, whose memory
calls up your ghost at cockcrow:
there and not there

if tears glister or no:

so, struck from your holy flesh,
                                        distance and
access, our words begin
                              like lepers' bells: O come
not near.

ATLAS

A fern at window
eyes
    the great-boned maple steadying for death. Cat

sat at a bullfight, and was bored.

Samson's falling
takes time
down with him:

greatness wears its lionheart and fleece.
He will never say it (say it!)
Good bye, manifestoes of summer love.
                                                  Atlas

take up the cross.

SAINT JOHN BAPTIST

I

    A sword forbade me to grow old; it cut
time like a parasite from eternity.

Could death have eyed and pierced my body, could I
have stood upon the nails an hour,
would he take warning from his murdered shade

casting his fate in smoky runes
with points of light
like lips where death had fastened?

I follow from sad limbo
till death unfasten, till his rising
unwind and wear me
aureole choir crown

II

In the mirror a sword made
descending
briefer than image a stream carries
beyond,
I saw John old: eyes cold, hair silver.

Look how I save you
sang the blade strongly:
dwarfing honors, prophecies by rote
a stalemate heart. Freedman, stand free.

I caught in two hands
this unripe storm-shaken fruit, by hate
(by love) tossed down
tasted at soul's root that wine's stream.

SAINT ANN

(who bore a daughter in late life)

Hand that folded and laid aside my fabric
as it pleased Him
when it pleased Him, shook me out,
billowed and filled me like a silken tent
A voice, He comes

shaking the women up
                                        at dawn, barefoot
through burning snow, and shouting *manna manna*

APOSTLES

Ringed Him about then,
not twelve profiles for a frieze.
Caesars, prophets, judges: would history have tossed
a rust coin on our future? doubt it.

No Moby, no conquistadors
but landmen groaning green on a two-mile pond
and He dry-shod as a Red-Sea Jew
cradling
distempered night to a babe's closed eye.

We grew gentle to harbor
Christ's dream of us
someday. Beached, and found
twelve dead men flung, wearing our faces drowned.

LAZARUS

Sister, you placed my heart in its stone room
where no flowers curiously come, and sun's voice
rebuffed, hangs on the stones dumb. What I could not bear
I still must hear. Why do your tears fall?

why does their falling move Him, the friend, the
unsuspected lightning: that He walk our garden
with no flowers upon His friend?

what did He say in tears (grief
scalding my hands, cold hands springing
sleep like a manacle) drawing my eyes a space
that had seen God, back to His human face?

SAINT PETER

A cock mounted the tall
rock where His body bled. I choose
that rock to stand: man
and clean of hand and blessed, whose
even second choice was Christ.

SAINT STEPHEN

That day stones fell
I died
unknowable, a mound of dust for heaven
to make man of.
That day stones beat
like stone beasts for a forced entry
to eat my heart: I prayed awhile
then opened brief and tossed them meat.
They ate and died of it: unproofed against
my living phial, great love.
That day
stones flew like hail of stones at first:
my dolorous flesh took their brute will
but stones transformed
to tongues, whispered at every wound:
welcome
That day stones flowered
to dark rose-field Christ walked and gathered.

SNOWMAN

The children wrapped up and skeined out and
rolled downhill death, who is ludicrous

but king too, from coal eyes surveying
from ruined mouth saying: *it is all like me*:

no blue or red of vein or heart
fired and set afoot, I do permit me.

The dwarf at shoulder, peering out of eyes
secret and simian, I do dispense with.

But head to boot one element, one temperate
cold requiring.
His fallen coals weep and are granted:
spare me sight of the unlike world, its hearts and

heats and blueveined ones

HEAR EVER SO GENTLY

Permanent beauty stands
nowhere under the tense
mainspring of time.

while I praise
color and voice of flowers
stealing my heart aside

so frail they are, this night's
starlit air has felled them.

The great cathedral takes
enemy year after year
deeper the spiritual thrust
on stained and wrinkled stone.

somewhere between its bones'
imperceptible wound
and the star-crossed flower

above a rust of bloom
under the doomed tower
hear: ever so gently

a main and springing hour

TREE: OCTOBER

under that summer cloud
whose rain is red and gold

around that vase's cunning
figures whom storm and calm
scatter to make again

about that summering swan
whose plumage winter hastens
away
      beneath those bells
whose beat broods on the air:

music, plumage, rain
whatever image hung

the great tree at heart

is fled   is flown   is spent
skeleton: element

MEN WERE THE IMAGE

Unlike a fish
that gestures feebly
with waving fronds from far back in time
I am still unborn
                    or a bat, blind
Icarus aground, limping in harness along:

trees confound death
by uprightness: they answer violence like a
gospel man:
                when storm made evident its brute will
and we, not falling to knee, rued dearly

who were the image? In calm a dance gesture,
in sorrow, joy. We shook night from limb
and stood: an arched instrument loud with them.

CHILD ABOVE A FLOWER

unsure
if he regards
or is regarded.
Both is a truth
older will fade.
Come, said flower
race me to evening.
Time is a way
no one knows.
Who
goes there?
who went there
answer our tears, sighs

flower's ghost. Growth is a death
on my youth laid.

MORE LIKE THE SEA

(A man is more than two sticks crossed.
He is more like the sea, bringing up God knows what
at any moment: Conrad)

Nail him to sticks
he stands free, makes sense
of agony, of sticks and stones.
No grafting him on: his fruits
are free, and other: more love
more year's intensities. He ranges, rejoices
the horizon sorrow lifts him to.

Look how hands refuse
all but gift. That blood will flow
red red against bitter
hemlock, maple sweet. Blood writes
what heart provides: God knows what
that sea brings up.

God bring that sea safe
—safe is no word for him-but a
surf home, shuddering its coast
crying hoarse in its falling
victory.

AN OLD WOMAN IN DEATH

For words words;
                                        death's instantaneous
waterfall
granted all at once
what sun fumbles weeks upon,
                                                            and only debatedly
brings to pass: I say spring

that springs her absent eyes:
like flowers whose seed dies in
temperate air, they fade here: but in height
elsewhere, are majestic blue

blue wept her eyes when she cried aloud:
in fear or exaltation, no one knows.
The woman who died
shook a worn garment aside

bride somewhere again
                                                by loving
                                                              makes beautiful.

WHICH WAY HUMAN?

Hemlocks in row, heads bowed beneath snowfall
like abstract old men, raven of hair once

but age is upon them: sorrow and reversal
in one night's course,
gently exhorted
into longsufferance by winter birds: in moonrise,
twilight, inching their shadow onward.
Eternity
is eventual: the trail sparse and
wavering: a star's flare, a wounded bird in snow:

vocation a ghost's cry: *which way* the human?

WE LOVE

about trees: past is never tall enough,
future too tall. Another spring will tell.

Tell another spring
I will be there, and fairer.
I become myself
that throat of swan
that striding giant I decree myself.

We love: in trees, in us, how many die
forward on the blade.
I see men like forests
striding, like swans riding, always
royally: though lowly afoot, striding into death.

What we love: there are not blades enough

GO DOWN ON KNEE

I saw an old wife stricken, the man
bending painfully above: *let me serve, be
eyes, limbs.*

Man, wife, wearing for better for
worse, the other's flesh, rent and patch: *I do.*
Bridal gown is yellow as bone, raveled

like youth out many a gay and slower
mile: stained bowler and waistcoat, a
rusty charmer.
Yet all days since, I see
visible things of this world, faultless
and heartening, go down on knee before, fashion
music toward, measure hope and
decline upon
the least audible heartbeat
of this holy darkness: *I love you.*

A STATUE OF THE BLESSED VIRGIN, CARVED IN WOOD

Wood is noble when it forgets resemblance

and like the first idea of tree
stands straight up and awaits creation.

Then art is arbitrary; it decrees

what moment Mary will pause in. Forbidding
lips their sound, shapes a phrase
of universal mercy. And the delicate outthrust foot
protests and starts: you are my errand.

LOVE IS A DIFFERENCE

Water is the shaping form whose blade
cuts
fish to jeweled finish.
Out of native air
we, soon lost.

But lends reason to,
whispers *here and now* to
air cut to a profile:

as a bell lifts
to pour on 4
winds their christening:
or majestic birds,
daring
a perilous clearing,
teach light its spectrum.

STRENGTH

issues in marvels:

crucial delicate finger at flute stop.

Hill easing itself like tiger's body, around one
blind tuft of violets.

A spring after, felled oak, one
heartbeat unspent: one
handful of leaves
in a dead hand.

BEETHOVEN'S VIOLIN

(for Carol and Jerry)

Birnam Wood across the plain, marches
season after season, into itself.
But the first day of all
dawns from that throat.

Tenderness and strength
do not dwell in one life.

Yet the violin
summons tears, commands action.
Its best face is a smile;
it is achieved, sings

fearfully and wonderfully made, sings
the violin. I have taken wings at morning
I have searched the uttermost sea: there is no one
to love me like this lover.
I am Eve, sings the violin:
I am taken from his side:
I heal with my body,
with sounds his hands make
the wound
I
opened
him.

3. The World for Wedding Ring

KINDER TIMES?

But what use were angels
in the raw world? Christ's hands and heart
time hammered open.
He pours
human over us. Breathe deep, question his wounds
what way now?

Listen; the chime, the synonym
made death a wine, turned all His body rose.

HE PAUSED

and spoke: *coopers, craftsmen, shepherds*
blessed is the prophet
whose blood speaks in his stead. Search death out

and sought death in their cities, and was taken
young years and all, composed in ground
like wintering bees

and after respite stood again
in tremendous mime, (shut doors sprung,
permeable world)
all we would come to.

DEATH CASTS NO LIGHT ON THE MIND

It is not for that; not
permeable at all, an Easter cross.

He crossed himself, and climbed

Then then

imagination springs; it tastes
mulberries, risen tigers, Himalayas,
summer lightning—

He leaped eternity
(whisper goes),
                a tiger to its prey.

SAINT MATTHEW, PUBLICAN

Caesar's coin
tastes no death. Turning full face
it lies full in face. *No god but Caesar*
says the gold eye that lights, like hell
nothing to buy.

Follow Me. Superscription, face
are sallow rust, a ruin
graves, armies, ignorant time
conspire toward. Caesar weeps at last
        at last, long lives.

HOPE

All night the fretful cricket

skirrs like a conscience, night in his bones
light in his points of eye—hope

illiterate and fey,
a cock raising minuscule dawn

match flare might make, or candle end
and he foolish cry *dawn!* at the false dawn

that wakened him for death.

How small a thing is hope—
hairspring body, mind's eye, and all endangered.

EVENTS

Events are orthodoxy, he would say,
submitting like any son.
The way a fruit tastes of itself
he tasted sacrifice.
No thirst but for that cup
engendering thirst.

Credo is event, would say
to a brother's face
by birth or death brought near—
a descending god he saw, a god
sprung from his tears.
Piety of experience
bound him in web.
He wore the world for wedding band.

Here
A few notes toward a life.
Words, words,   we buried.

Look; time wears new feature; time takes heart.

THE POEM WAITS ON EXPERIENCE

  a ghost in offstage darkness; no lines,
no wig, no eyes. I have not loved the poor,
I have not died yet.

Yet I am poor
as all the shanties of the world
gone up in flares;

on a rotted springs
a junky's baked skeleton.

Here, for its worth, the poem.

THE POET AS OBSERVER

I sit like a dunce in the incandescent noon
stool, cap, notes

a liberated blind man
whose eyes bear him like wings
out of night's stinking nest, into this world.

Intellectual vision, reality by definition?
No. The Jesuit mind, a Homer

assembles fleets, sails for its continent
across seas tamed by the ordering governing glance.

But to light on and finger the world, bit by bit
an old woman in a flea market—

junk, onions, ordure. Ingredients and parts.
The old fingers, wise as eyes, come on something. A yes.

TO WALLACE STEVENS

In each of us you live on, the lodged seed
of empiric imagination
from a great pod blown on death's virile wind.

Credo, we said, *credo,* mirror
to mirror, an inhumanity
before no god.

You are our puzzle. You, naked as we
amid the poverties of our world

—flowers, donkeys, angels meek as water—
cunningly
surpassed us in an hour. Refusing our credo
your marvelous method
made dawn, made a world, made marriage of light and flesh

without God, you said. But is decree of absence
final, when the imagination yields
like a god's brow
godlike humans, armed, passionate for their world?

1961

I summon my parents, a jubilee morning.
When in gold vestments I came down
to kiss them where they stood, their tears and mine

were a clear pressing of the eighty-year vine.
I touched their faces, a gentle unweathered grain
the blind might visualize, as of green leaves
up from exposed ground.
What winter fury
that moment tempered, they and I know.

HOMILY

Said; a cleric worth his salt
will salt his bread with tears, sometimes.
will break bread
which is the world's flesh, with the world's poor,
count this his privilege and more—

And called Saint Paul for exemplar
whose fingers stitched the church a robe,
its crude device
a Christ crucified, wrought of his workman's hands

which the foul dust had sealed
utter and unforeseen, priest and lord.

No disdain must stain the workman's hands
that such task own
It is all one, I cried. The Lord
upbears the poor man's hand in His, His fruit.
Gospel has it so; one, grape, tendril, shoot and root.

The confession of humanity is our honor, clerics.
Celibate, father—that irony
time urges to term—
You are the poor man's food.
Or great Burgundy, rotting, sours time's ground.

GOOD CAIPHAS

perfumes, resin, nard—
they fell in showers
on fallen Christ.
We will make sandalwood of him
and store like bees
honey in his stern eyes.
Someone, ages gone
will touch a spring
and chant the open-sesame
and find our golden Pharaoh safe as wheat.

Or so they thought.
But blood, blood
writes red
one name, when dawn breaks
it wakens, and we cry—
is this the wasted vine
God's hand has healed, pressed, poured?

Flesh too from one dark loom
is ours and his, whole cloth.

When winds take him on high
we follow too.
That watchful hurrying prince's eye
sails us to the Father.

THE FACE OF CHRIST

The tragic beauty of the face of Christ
shines in our faces;

the abandoned old live on
in shabby rooms, far from comfort.
Outside,
din and purpose, the world, a fiery animal
reined in by youth. Within
a pallid tiring heart
shuffles about its dwelling.

Nothing, so little, comes of life's promise.
Of broken, despised minds
what does one make—
a roadside show, a graveyard of the heart?

Christ, fowler of street and hedgerow
cripples, the distempered old
—eyes blind as woodknots,
tongues tight as immigrants'—all
taken in His gospel net,
the hue and cry of existence.

Heaven, of such imperfection,
wary, ravaged, wild?

Yes. Compel them in.

IRONIES

Ironies
draw the mind free of habitual
animal ease. Sough of tides in the heart,
massive and moony, is not our sound.

But hope and despair together
bring tears to face, are a human ground,
death mask and comic, such speech
as hero and commoner devise, makes sense

contrive our face. To expunge
either, is to cast snares for the
ghost a glancing heart makes
along a ground, and airy goes its way.

NOT YET

I remember this;
hands of Christ laid
across brow and eyes.
The man of action stilled,
a single vein
named thought, named love
reaming him through.

Christ and Mary know me
true grain and crooked, one.
She turning eyes from Him, as Beatrice once
bestows infrequently
a glance brimming with Christ.
And flaming souls tongue
mother and son draw near!

but here
purgation and afar

TERESA OF AVILA

Almighty God could make again
did malice unmake the world
from my turning heart, a world of use enough.

When I ride under moon, it is
in love in love frosty wheels sing.

Profiles, trades, brogues, oxen
milk-white, hillsides
holding, still as old shepherds, valleys of lambs—

a universe His majesty had not
foreseen? seed, pollen, world
by what gravity drawn, by wind driven,
nest in this dun body,
burr to my heart.

LANDSCAPES THERE ARE

of formal will and silken atmosphere;
where is the legendary Chinese brush
drawing us
gently into stillness?

Not conquest of height
nor grandiose will
but an uncopyable phrase

a bough in one direction
running.
Like a child's legend or a death
or *I love you*, never in history repeating itself.

THE EFFORT OF UNDERSTANDING

Look up.
To claim the air as that hawk does—
fatuous image.

At such height, earth is a poor
glomerate of no smells, no elbows.
                                        I had rather

here.

                        But there
catch breath, sometimes;
what does he, what would I, know?

A STATUE OF THE BLESSED VIRGIN, CARVED IN IVORY

Such a curve time grew;
at viable tip of inauspicious starts
is you.
        The race strives to bear,
                                    a Swedish

fountain-piece,
sons and daughters
upward,
        like waters,
                        in hope of you.

THE LEVITE

(a ninth-century crucified, Metropolitan Museum)

A thousand-year-old corpse has no redress;
undistracted, head upon breast

In that confessional guise, all is his grist

whose blood is rust, whose body
clings like a locust shell its tree.

We read the image. One Friday
one hour, signatory

of guilt and guilt expunged; we
roundelay about this pole

airing an argument which unopposed
we win, you lose.

Simply, though under wormwood
under old nails and joists, under

a stroke of ancient style that isolates
(time's genius) your visionary gift—

compounded, a calculus of time—

yet, we beseech, have done
let the pierced arms have done

stretched loins, drained heart, all
their tragic charade. The dead may come

their task done, into resurrection—
an hour, a transcendent hush

a stranger's face at door, a voice,
unfaltering hands, our evening bread.

AWAKENING

When I grew appalled by love
and stood, a sick man
on feeble knees
peering at walls and weather
the strange outdoors, the house of strangers—
there, there was a beginning.

The world peeled away
usual upon usual
like foil in a fire.
Fell that day, all summer
That day, mind made an elegy
world might gape and weep.

I forget it now.
But remember too; a green tree
all winter's ignorant winds trampled in vain.

HAVING ENDURED THE DEAD

(for Tony Walsh)

who without hands trouble the latch
who without sight
darken the world's fraudulent show

having endured the dead

who without tongue moil the night's lust
laugh it to black scorn

having endured the dead.

Last night Russ Whalen's death
struck us in face, his friends.

You bore it hardest, who dwell for years
on rotting Young Street. *Poor man*
the poor name you; they forgive
Christ for your sake.

Behind a crooked shutter
death's blear look
takes your measure too, waiting day out.

DEATHBED

Failure of action was that hour's loss.
Mind had its empyrean
fastidious, cleaner than bone
he came and went, our doors and minds assaulting

with lordly assumption; *you may*
if it please you, stand idle as park statues
casting cold tears
on dogs or the rotting poor. Not I.

And so resigned the world. For what world
what hands contrived, by what means fending—

Like dogs or the poor, he said.

Failure of heart, they said.

SAINT PETER SPEAKS

Neither prideful nor superhuman—
a racked man
a haunted man, better;
far from false heart
and big promissory words.

Hands articulate
in stillness or action;

another face among faces
in twilight; out of whose body
emanations, uses of work and love
streamed like night mist
up from earth. A racked man,
a haunted man, I knew him.
If God put on a country face,

hefted gear, wrung
like any son, sustenance from his acre—

all were in this image,
intent, hereditary, skillful
an unmistaking wit

Mazed by courtesies
multiplied in secret,
I had forgotten
the numbed bewilderment
that stole our wits
at the violent end.

But think now to recover
semblance of order
from that willful disordered murder.
I remember Tiberias sea
storming straight up
at the wind's trump.
On that green hell one face appears
sunken, nearing its peace, then clearer.

He walked the storm. He made peace be.
He summoned me, as though sea
were road and rest, Himself.
Racked man, haunted man—
the saving pain of life
is to drown out of one's human
stinking corpse,
a taken foolish fish
at wit's end drawn into being.

MY MOTHER

I know love's
are large claims, but hers
modest

as hands;
a word, a flower,
a child's face for instrument.

Even in dreams, hands speak
Speak?
Creation is summons.
Their speech creates
awakenings.

PARABLE

Cripples died at pool side,
in roadways, ditches, porches.
No help for it.

And if by crutch or crook one stood—
a most unsettling genius;

delays, deferring eyes;
superior vision

declined. No miracle.

No *why.* Death kept a close mouth.

LAZARUS

I

Silence rolled over, over my body its
monstrous milling; a fine dust
settled on millstone death.

If truth were told, the white dust could not tell it
even when that young Magian
cried *open-sesame* and puffed me to a man.

II

After my world was only
two women above me, and they murmuring
gradual farewell, like bells or heartbeat—

I could not care, nor summon
to whisper *I do not care.* Yet for them
heart stood like a stricken drummer: one beat more.

*It was not death!*Though his steps slower fell than the great stone,
he cried; *I am the way*

and banished death away
chiding
from the stone doorway
away
their tears.

4. No One Walks Waters

HOLY WEEK, 1965

(North Vietnam: the air raids go on)

For us to make a choice
was always a wrong choice—
why not die in the world
one was born into? what was wrong?

They were patient almost as time.
Their words ate like a tooth.

They looked into our eyes
wild by starts, like the times.
They saw
and marveled, and shook. We saw
out of the edge of the eye
hell;
        out of the center eye
a command. And blinked
their asperges away; *be blind.*

THE WRITING OF A POEM

Greatness of art
is a newborn look, a cry

or the gaze
the dying summon toward the newborn
held before clouding eyes,
a flagon, the unpoured cup of going.

Too sorrowful? say then
greatness is exclusions,
(totems, weights, measures,
woodbins, diets,
midnight arrogance of clocks,
the cat's somnolent metaphysic—

see with a spot I damn them.)

The greatness of art; it cries *reality!*
like a mordant blinded god.

KEEP THE HOUR

I set this down toward May midnight.
A blind moon in search of intellect
walks the waste sky in vain. But listen—

the wild kildeer, deprived, importunate
cries out: *you, you are my passion.*

Enough, all said—
the mind's life, so ironic victory
in a stark hour.

YOU FINISH IT: I CAN'T

The world is somewhere visibly round,
perfectly lighted, firm, free in space,

but why we die like kings or
sick animals, why tears stand
in living faces, why one forgets

the color of the eyes of the dead—

WE ARE IN LOVE, THE CELIBATES GRAVELY SAY

They hold Christ up
like athletes at a trampoline, but

if I go, I return He says
skilled in gravity

His continuing declension
like dew or fiery napalm

or the seeding of streams with trout eggs.
The earnest orantes hold their hands

safe as stone up to the absent One
which He presently strikes, forges and fills—

world, and world's beauty.

THE QUESTION

If the world's temperate zone,
then too
its cruel weather,
punishing torrid, arctic.

If freedom, then two wills
conflicting; wild Cain,
smooth-phrased Abel, too good
for foul actual life.

If shelter for sad shepherd,
then the wild verge of the heart,
extravagance, violence; the lamb
murdered; rot and stench.

If the way,
then no way at all; way lost
last chance, a Potter's waste.

If fiery vine, then sour lees at heart.

If silence, forbearance
under all malice—

O when
when will You have done
imagining?

MIRACLES

Were I God almighty, I would ordain,
rain fall lightly where old men trod,
no death in childbirth, neither infant nor mother,
ditches firm fenced against the errant blind,
aircraft come to ground like any feather.

No mischance, malice, knives.
Tears dried. Would resolve all
flaw and blockage of mind
that makes us mad, sets lives awry.

So I pray, under
the sign of the world's murder, the ruined son;
why are you silent?
feverish as lions
hear us in the world,
caged, devoid of hope.

Still, some redress and healing.
The hand of an old woman
turns gospel page;
it flares up gently, the sudden tears of Christ.

AIR TRIP TO BOSTON

(a priest, Connolly, ordained near death)

1.

I may become
sharp tongued, intolerant, a sore old man.
It looks as though, sometimes.

Still, have stolen from Rouault's art
the old king's fragile unkillable flower.

Heal-all, sweeten my mind's stream.

2.

Turning a page
I came on your death, Connolly,
the fierce crawl of time
a dragged limb or cross.
Then, your hollowed brows
five, ten years before—
no eyes or face, no particulars.

Rain wash, wind wash, wash of time!
The brow, a bowl
ground perfect on the earth's wheel

for holding of—what? You, empty, know.

3.

The long line of birches—
landing among them at the airstrip edge,
Russian bells or Saint Elmo's fire
or the plumage of swans;
                                        one voice
flooding the senses
making truth of the world; *start with us!*

A PITTSBURGH BEGGAR REMINDS ME OF THE DEAD OF HIROSHIMA

Seeing the beggar's sign
lettered and hung like a sandwich board—
"I am blind, suffer from angina
and claim no pension or support of any kind."

the crowd dug deep, the tin can
sang like a wishing well.

These days, everyone being at war,
not to pay dear is to prod the inner horror
awake; speech starting up by heart,
lights going on and off, a Greek sky
where five stars make a god; a voice
we got them there; or *he stood like a bastard here, but*
we took him piece by piece;
shipped his skull home, polished like a gouty
whole head—

Perhaps the poem is odd man out
wherein my foulness
drags forward, touches His flesh
an emperor's birthmark
under beggardry, leprosy.
I am too unschooled to know,
befouled and blinded by the hot droppings
that struck my eyes in sleep, from the great bird
the descending fecal horror.
I stood and shook like ague
—Hiroshima, Nagasaki—
the ungentle names of my memory's youth,
the blue remembered hills
tipping like hell's buckets all their
hot afterbirth on me.

Healer, you would need
stout heart where I must stand;
no bones, nothing to start with
for repair and solace
of thc vast meridian horror.
You would peer and poke
a blind man on a dump
tracing—another stone in a
dismembered wall—the Neanderthal
boy's bones, half discernible

in turned-up garden litter,
the obliterated dead, the slight
rhythms of marble tracery or flesh—which?

I believe in the Father almighty
and in Jesus Christ
his risen flesh, indistinguishable
from the permeating stench
that rises, spreads, drifts
on prevailing island winds
when a people goes up, a
mockup of city
slapped together for a brief
sequence—*lights, drone, target*—

Flesh of Christ—
indistinguishable, compounded
yeast, seed, flowering
of human flesh
your healing starts here
with the tears the dead
were given no time for, the living
numbed, no heart for.

You, Lazarus, who died and stank—
stagger like a zombie
out of the rubble, jaws
like a burnt carp, unfit for
speech or kiss, that fed
three days down, on carrion death.

Be first. Arise.
Teach the dead their discipline
—shank, hair, ear, articulation—
that rode like furies the inner seas
or fell
a dew on fleece, or settled
like sandman's gifts
on the eyes of sleeping children.

I toss a coin in the wishing
flesh of beggars; coins in the eyes
of murdered children, for buying of
no tears; a coin
in the carp's mouth for Peter's cast.

The dead too; my coin stand you in stead
who went improvident,
no staff or shift, into time's mountain
as though all
were wide door; this momentary hell
a heaven, and passing fair.

CLUNY MUSEUM

The woman's hands weave
shroud or birth clout in air;
a homely face, a woman
not of any countryside I have seen;
a servant perhaps, bowed
with night or dawn labors. And now this death—
hearthstone cold, the beloved son
the single and perfect fruit, crushed under heel.

But a tragic woman stands firm for others' sake.
There is crowding of life on her,
even the dead give place. She stands so.

The living son stands too, as this
wooden man stuck through
with a murderous spike, cannot know. Come,
I touch his wood. A wildfire; Rise,
the Lord is risen.

FOUNTAINHEAD

The open well
collects leaves, waste, vanities;

then, under hands
water runs free again
tideless, endlessly yielding

a cold spring
blessed by wayfaring gods

Hands hold the world in cleft
where waters are born;
lucid, living, a murmurous child.

COMPASSION

I sing bronze statuary
enduring rain and cold,
alert eyes casting back
the sun's burning shafts
a fisher's net soaring,
snare
to catch worlds in.

But in November rain
—rotting asters, scum of leaf—
came on a dying man.

His eyes pled
like an animal at the block
Come to this? And I
kneel upon squalid ground
defeat striking
marrow and heart;
Unless I suffer this, you
gentlest Abel, strike
with a glance, Cain down.

MAKING SOMETHING

The blind man
longed passionately to see

but wish was vain
while dawn delayed
a false savior, no sight
from his miraculous store.

The cripple dreamed
dancers and tumblers all night long; at dawn
lay there, dumb
as the world's wood or winter,
no volcanic man.

Tears are an only poem.
I spread out
like a blind fakir, on the mat of the mind
sorry magic;
two scored stones for eyes,
broken sticks for limbs;
for man—
sans eyes, sans hands, a century's
empty locust shell
For oracle, only
be content, be like.

POPE PAUL GOES TO JERUSALEM; THE MONA LISA AND THE PIETÀ GO TO NEW YORK

If geography's the tip of someone's
scholastic needle, we'll ripen and rot there.
But life? Mona Lisa tries her luck
in treacherous waters. The innocuous stare

warms, her body cleaves the waters
like time's ripe swan. And Pieta, too long

in stale unanswering air; *whose sorrow*
like mine? Lady, we've not lived as long

in churches, but we die too, in droves.
In Queens meadow raise your eyes
from classic grief. The dead
bury the dead, and deep. Come walk our streets. Like Paul

the sun almost destroyed, that white moth.
He sweated under the cross, the raving
combustible crowd, a hanging or crowning mood.
In dreams, the living eat his flesh, his blood runs
nightlong a staved cask in those alleys.

My dream beats on. I see the dead
in naked majesty, consumed with longing
for what we in the common street have by heart;
the leaf's errant fall, a child's cry. Delicate,
  brutal; impure, pure-the world, the world—
  breaks them apart.

HIS CLERIC'S EYE
(G.M.)

A young priest, dead suddenly
at forty years
taught a metaphysic of the world.
His mind was lucid, ingrained. He would say,
it is deductibly verified
that God is immutable; and,
universal order converges on one being.

So be it. This priest, alas for poetry, love and priests
was neither great nor evil.
The truths he spoke
being inert, fired no mind to a flare;
a remote world order

of essence, cause, finality,
invited submission to his God.

He never conveyed a man, Christ, or himself—
His cleric's eye
forbade singulars, oddments, smells,
sickness, pushcarts, the poor.
He dwelt in the fierce Bronx, among a university's
stone faced acres
hemmed in by trucks and tumbrels. No avail.

Yet it could not be borne
by those who love him, that having passed
from unawareness to light
he should be denied
the suffering that marks man
like a circumcision, like unstarched tears; *saved.*

Heaven is everything earth has withheld.
I wish you, priest, for herald angel,
a phthisic old man
beating a tin can with a mutton bone—
behold he comes!

For savior,
a Coxey's army, a Bowery 2 A.M.
For beatific vision
an end to books, book ends, unbending minds,
tasteless fodder, restrictive order.

For eternal joy
veins casting off, in a moment's
burning transfiguration
the waste and sludge of unrealized time.

Christ make most of you!
stitch you through
the needle's eye, the grudging gate.
Crawl through

that crotch of being;
new eyes, new heart, the runner's burning start.

AND HE FED THEM ALL

That throng
Christ had worked wonders for—

The gentle blind
hearing like fauns
the fall of leaf, the hunters mindless will—

the halt
like marvelous broken statuary;

they come for eucharist, as though rumor ran
in grim autumnal streets
long cold, long unfed

of miraculous loaves and fishes among the dead.

TALISMAN

I wear
for sign of debt
a silver medal of Christ
sterile of flower or word,
itself time's flower
molten and hard; face incised
in the years' acid,
a savior's eye
sleepless, surviving.

I wear it, a weakling
who kisses the knees of the warrior he fears
and in the dust, may yet
arise to love.

The face turns full profile away—
from time's stinking silver, Judas' kiss?

But a chain swings the rabbi full about.
The face is become
a savior's change of heart.
He turns to me.
I may yet
if silver outlast flesh

die unhanged in bed,
bought, sold for silver.

IF

If I am not built up
bone upon bone
of the long reach and stride of love—

if not of that
as stars are of their night;
as speech, of birth and death; thought
a subtle paternity, of mind's eye—

if not, nothing.
A ghost costs nothing.
Casts nothing, either; no net,
no fish or failure, no tears like bells

summoning across seas
the long reach and stride of love
dawning, drowning those black waters.

I ENCOUNTER MEN IN THE WORLD

hopelessness stands in their eyes,
dry despair, hands broken upon stones,
eroded lives

I think then, of a young mother
her child in arms
a concentrated inwardness
as of a sea shell coiled, its music
self-composed, self-given.

I long at sight of illness to induce
—as a shell drawn from seas
generative, uncorrupted—
some birth their tears had not dared come upon.

THE SISTINE CHAPEL

Illusory, a maelstrom of wrong purpose.
I would whitewash the whole.
Then, in favor of religion,
place there
for a poverello's sake
for his gospel eye, Cezanne's *Card Players*, say.

See, the painter cries, *God*
is that meditative peasant
or the watcher brooding over; He is
like us, all said.

Divine things
need only look human. The cards deal and fall
fair as leaves or creation; we are in good hands.

SORROW

I saw a mother
mourning her sick child
the hundredth time that day
or any day or night
equally wearying, equally hopeless.
She sees death stand at the end of days.

And saw a young husband;
his wife, suddenly dead, borne to the church door,
he, serving at Mass
impassive, cold at wrist and heart
to match her cold, one ice laid on one flesh.

The exemplary world moves us to tears
that in their falling, purify
eye's glance, impure world, both.

I know the world now, if world has face.
It beats steadily as a child's heart.
It is the moon's rhythm
that like a woman's long
unutterable glance of love
draws the bridegroom after.

SONG

(from Jacopone Da Todi)

In my morning prayer
I saw *love* written
upon every creature

men on their foreheads
trees on their leaves
houses on their walls.

Christ has flowered in flesh
let human nature rejoice!

PRAGUE: OLD WOMAN IN THE STREET

In the country saying, she was only
doing what must be done, as a stone falls

or a wheel turns; punished
by a man's labor, to man's shape.

Childbearing done, not for twilight peace
but for this; pulling a cart, sweeping cobbles
stolid in the killing cold. Suffering?
hands were made for it, blood warmed to it.

I tell you, I stood stupefied
as though a flare went up in the foul street,
some ikon Christ casting rags off for glory.

Woman I never knew, I kneel,
I am born of you. For you, my heart keeps
like an unhealed leper's, stint of hope—

Christ is not hard as stone, cold as my doubt.
You neared. Unbearably, the quick dead cried out.

MOMENT

Is the world then, more
than an animal haunch, cleft
under the butcher's ax,
a world hung raw, flayed on a hook?

Is the world more? is it
five or six deer together, standing in dusk
abstract, momentary; then startled, dissolved in
newer and newer rhythms, mauve hoofs, red nostils
eyes unwary as first stars?

Are we, the watchers
bathed in that sight, a baptism?
The world
for all its stern exactions, loved us once:

homeward in dark, pondering *what is the world?*

A YOUNG BIRD FOUND DYING, BROUGHT INDOORS

The bird
never mastered air, and of earth
drew in no health, but a foul humor—
now lies blackening
and dead childish thing
untried by the world.

Earth mother—
tender, plangent, taking all to breast,
(children, great heroes, beauty, intellect)—

so slight a soul
lies light in a ghost's hand. Grant it
breath, passage to morning;
a furious phoenix brightening of hell

DACHAU IS NOW OPEN FOR VISITORS

The arabesque scrawled by the dead
in their laborious passage,
leaf and flower mould of their spent bodies,
faces frost touches
gently and coldly
to time's geometric—

a multitude   skeletons
press   forward; such cries
the patient poor speak whose despair
leaves no peace intact, no coin
for death's foreclosing fist.

I FEAR MOST, I THINK

if nightmare is oracle—
not madman death

not quartan fevers
nor the long litany hell composes
of unstrung jaws, their fiery diatribe

but dreaming or waking—
that child
pale as mushroom, blind as night fog

no grace, no stance, no name—
shuddering, lame, befouling the world.

IN THE CHILDREN'S WARD

I was pondering no mystery
and far in mind from mystery's
Necromancer who, time gone,
made five flowers grow
in consecrated ground,
lit five candles in a ghost's hands and feet.

Merciful, men and women stood apalled
when the Lord sank and died; a crowned head
must, if it rise intact
make a fiery circle around; all
stand without.

I thought as I bent
to innocent blind faces
how inmost sight refused my face; linen
ripped like graverot; eyes
no tears burned black, met mine.
And pity died—the feeble child
my childish nightmare made
of rickety bed and doll.

All, all wrong.
Sight was blind. But the children

moved dexterous as fireflies, in a blind
garden of broken hands and dull minds

PARIS SUITE

1. A BEGGAR, FIRST

Sometimes, misery has beauty to commend it.
I saw a poor man bedding down
in the midnight street, coolly. He might have been
gorgeous Louis preparing levee.

Weather stood austere,
late goers homeward, pinched, intent.
The beggar made his bed as best
rags, leaves, torn paper might. De Gaulle's

disgruntled snowman face
crumpled under head, made a pillow
like ambergris
floating the brain gently nightlong

in a grand savory sauce
of power and rhetoric. Human life
flickers inextinguishably in the jungle street.
The beggar, annealed in dignity

settles back
in rags his dignity weaves new.
He takes up in cold hands
tattered Molière: Those cunning civilized hands

that lifted, veil on veil
the quintessential ironies of mind,
that fleeced the rich to very clout, that hailed
great Jove in rags—

        crown him at midnight.

2. OUR LADY OF PARIS

Mother of exodus, her cold hands take
of this world no comfort

Tonight, stinking Seine
leaps the quay stones, takes living flesh
in morsels. A gypsy
mother and child might dream
four walls and fire; and Mary
white faced at door for shelter.
Always, the poor—

Dives screams in his stews,
his tripod of burning bones.

3. CONCESSIONS

You are not the golden Greek sea, no
Shakespeare never slept here—
granted, the nightingale is heard
only in Versailles tapestry;

starting with stern exclusions
I end as always
helpless in praise;
marvelous architect of humans, mind's life that
transubstantiates to poetry.

Cast words away. The city, the
egg of Venus, halves into all things.

4. SAINT SULPICE

In the botched barracks, coming on
a marvelous suave Christ; thigh to wrist, one line
of contending death and life, the wood
golden as time's honeycomb—
                                        stuck out of sight for
being guilty of beauty
                              as though in some

grimy back yard, a scarecrow stood
and withstood, and in spring arose
caparisoned as Spring Christ with trumpet vine.

5. UNFINISHED LINES

A bronze head of Mallarmé by Picasso—
the true burden of falling leaves.
Do humans live only in thought? Where are their hands?
Why ask? Great lines crown the brow
that crowns its quiet grove.

But how clasp hands with the dismembered dead?

No one's familiar. Listen and look long.

6. PARIS, YOU COULD PRESS WINE FROM THISTLES

make easter eggs of gutter stones.
Your metaphysical butchers chop and chop,
time's neat headsmen. Irony and grace
hold like a lifted shrug, all life in fee.

What unlikely thing is not your poem?
One leaf in Luxembourg gardens
trodden, dried, a simian brown.
But hold it up; a fan, a lover's lattice
to say through to the world
if you stand there in brown twilight, I love you.

7. A VIEW FROM A SIDE STREET

The streets
shouldering awkwardly along

like flower carts
all sight and bestowal—

windows like blank eyes
starved
for one burning realizing blue—

Walk out
some night
                that sacks your sight,
a condemned man's,
                                in suffocating black

Be lucky,
            a star falls,
                        cry out *I see.*

8. A THRUSH IN THE CITY

Supple as a fish
or a violinist's hands
the thrush
fans out, ascends,
paying to gravity
the tribute of grace

not as a parasite
I drink of you earth mother
but standing at height
to pour from a gold mask
poetry on your wounds

9. THE CITY UNDERTAKES A RESTORATION OF PUBLIC MONUMENTS

To admit death and beginning

taking that blow like any woman
her brow wet
with birth or death sweat, she scarce
knows. *How much life?* she mocks death

I would in the wandering city
make in my mind that phrase
new, anew; despite
time's cruelties, that belabor

innocent clear expectancies.
How much life? I seek.
Algerian workers
with steam hoses, burnish new
the scarred animate bones of Paris.

10. THE NEWSTAND

In cold November
the old man stood
all day
in a flimsy canvas box,
struts, patches;
                a lung, a world
billowing with big portentous names.
The stone man stood;
                drumming like a god
wars, death,
            time's bloodletting and getting.

At sundown
                the world came apart,
a shack of cloth and board
                            roped, hefted.
Last, rolled up his pages;
                            the leonine faces
snuffed without cry,
                        dead as all day.

11. IMMANENCE

I see You in the world—
venturesome children, their cries and gestures,
the sharp sad whistle at six, the emptying park,
flybitten leaves, embers of the magnificent
weathered candelabra, the poplar lanes.

Yet faith asks, like a shaky woman, some epiphany—
a renaissance cock calling Peter's sin

from the Pantheon roof, shocking the crowd's ease,
sinking the children's fleet

that now make alas, as life does, a silly wayward wake
or none at all; and no one walks waters.

12. AIR MAIL LETTER

That mysterious lord
ikons and saints speak of
seldom if ever deigns
miracles, interventions.

I saw once, a procession
of halt, blind nuns;
on Corpus Christi day
they wove of flowers and leaves
their *tao*, their adoration

Dark fell; the nuns'
bodies swung like vanes.
Their eyes
triumphant, ravaged, held
life's acid ironies.

I carried the Host that day.
They in the doorway singing
floated midstream;
a foil of swanlike forms

Then
(no warning)
steeled upright, turned
intent, unappeased, to me.
Come cried the virgins *despise*
vain emulation, the childish
time-ridden heart. Bring to birth
in one flush of being
intelligence and love.

The moment passed. Twelve
defeated women, singing
Pange Lingua. Slowly
entered again the dark
portal of horn or ivory.

These occurred to me—
gentle adherence, love,
hope beyond reason of hope.

THE POEM

When I see flowers borne into a city room
I am urged inward—
the gross slag, filth and mire
to the heart of life.

Amplitude, warmth, saving grace—
the flowers beat and beat on. The divine ship,
silken and tough in the wind,
beats and beats on. The poem—
   the journey toward.

5. Love, Love at the End

PRAYER OF THE VINDICATED

Thank you at last. The question indeed
was long and vexed, allowing
                this or that stab at solution
                  in long run unavailing.

Then the state gathered strength out of weakness,
a dynastic leopard starved itself for the feast.
A people known in the world
For coals, gases, alkaloids, engines, boots
and amenities more precise and cunning—
false teeth, false hair, the reprocessing of
old bones and bottles, melting down of jewelry—
a genius to make the head spin in the telling!

Well, we were a chosen people
once more chosen! The gears ground fine
the fires were stoked. Our children
included
in the vast 'definitive solution',
swept along, a minor debris—shoes, scraps of clothing,
a scrawled diary—in the universal tide,
crying like caged birds
at the railroad sidings,
shoved like matzoth trays
into the ovens.

We came too, cajoled
to the same ruin. The smoke stood up
here and there in the faultness sky, a ghetto baking
before sabbath eve.

Chosen! the winch squeals like a tortured
animal, the wine press oozes red.
Chosen! the rings stripped from the womens' fingers,
the mailed bridegroom; Jahweh, our God a consuming
        fire!

SUBURBAN PRAYER

Grant us for grace
oppositions, stimyings
sand in our pet gears
a bubble in the cozy blood

Crowd our real estate
with the rag tag real, the world.
Marry us off, lonely girls
to Harlem and Asia. This Lent
celebrate in the haunted house, the world.

PRAYER ON THE SIX P.M. SUBWAY

unsteady
my prayer mounts or falls   why do I
waste so   want so
O make room
in the kingdom of light for lack lusters
among the austere and severe
for malfunction.
only this to their crediters NO GREAT HARM DONE
our passage writes
MAYBE on water

nevertheless
might make it yet
who knows who knows
whether some hour
turns us on
unbelievable
as Christ's new somersaulting
start.   his words   his heart

PRAYER FROM A WHITE SKIN

Where we have lighted
the rehearsing fires of hell

let a tear
from the furious eye of the poor
fall, extinguishing.
Unwind unwind
the cerements that bind
Lazarus
hand and foot in his flesh
his guilt large
on absurd phylacteries;
skin win white right.
A black face rives the stone
"*COME FORTH TO THE LORD'S DAY.*"

PRAYER FROM A PICKET LINE

Bring the big guardian
angels or devils in black
jackets and white casques
into the act at last. *Love, love at the end.*

The landholders withholding
no more; the jails springing
black and white Easter men;
truncheons like lilies, hoses
gentle as baby pee. *Love, love at the end.*

Bishops down in the ranks
mayors making it too.
Sheriff meek as a shorn lamb
smelling like daisies, drinking dew.
Love, love at the end.

PRAYER FOR THE MORNING HEADLINES

MERCIFULLY GRANT PEACE IN OUR DAYS. THROUGH YOUR HELP MAY WE BE FREED FROM PRESENT DISTRESS . . . HAVE MERCY ON

WOMEN AND CHILDREN HOMELESS IN FOUL WEATHER, RANTING LIKE BEES AMONG GUTTED BARNS AND STILES. HAVE MERCY ON THOSE (LIKE US) CLINGING ONE TO ANOTHER UNDER FIRE, TERROR ON TERROR, GRAPES THE GRAPE SHOT STRIKES. HAVE MERCY ON THE DEAD, BEFOULED, TRODDEN LIKE SNOW IN HEDCES AND THICKETS. HAVE MERCY, DEAD MAN, WHOSE GRANDIOSE GENTLE HOPE DIED ON THE WING, WHOSE BODY STOOD LIKE A TREE BETWEEN STRIKE AND FALL, STOOD LIKE A CRIPPLE ON HIS WOODEN CRUTCH. WE CRY: HALT! WE CRY: PASSWORD! DISHONORED HEART, REMEMBER AND REMIND, THE OPEN SESAME: FROM THERE TO HERE, FROM INNOCENCE TO US: HIROSHIMA DRESDEN GUERNICA SELMA SHARPEVILLE COVENTRY DACHAU. INTO OUR HISTORY, PASS! SEED HOPE. FLOWER PEACE.

PRAYER FOR THE BIG MORNING

People my heart
with the living! their cries like
fists, their sight healing
my eye's foreclosing night.
Would be
that one and populous
heart of man;
O cries like fists
O sight set free!

6. False Gods, Real Men

FALSE GODS, REAL MEN

1.

Our family moved in 25 years from Acceptable Ethnic
through Ideal American
        (4 sons at war   Africa   Italy   the Bulge   Germany)
and Ideal Catholic
        (2 sons priests   uncle priest   aunt nun   cousins
                great-uncle   etc.   etc.)
But now; 2 priests in and out of jail, spasms, evictions,
                confrontations

We haven't made a nickel on the newest war
probably never again
                will think, proper
with pride; a soldier! a priest! we've made it now!

What it all means is—what remains.
        My brother and I stand like the fences
            of abandoned farms, changed times
            too loosely webbed against
                deicide   homicide
A really powerful blow,
        would bring us down like scarecrows.
Nature, knowing this, finding us mildly useful
    indulging also
    her backhanded love of freakishness
                allows us to stand.

The implication
        both serious and comic;
            wit, courage
        a cry in the general loveless waste
        something

than miracle
  both more and less

. . . did conspire to enter, disrupt, destroy
draft files of the American Government,
on the 17 day of May . . .
—Indictment

2.

Among the flag poles
wrapped like Jansenist
conventicles
with rags
at half mast
(alas for sexual
mortmain) the wooden poles
on high but
dry

3.

We did yes we did your Honor
impenitent—
while legitimate cits
newts   bats   foxes
made congress
in formerly
parks and green swards
rutting   earnestly drilling
tooth and claw
galling   inserting
industrious   inventive
nitroglycerin, nuclear
instrumentalities

4.

We fools and felons
went on a picnic
apples   quince   wines   hams   swimsuits

loaves fishes noonday relics and traces
badminton watery footsoles infants all
thereafter impounded!

An FBI agent estimated at least 600 individual files were in the two huge wire baskets carried from Local Board No. 33 and set fire in the parking lot.

—AP dispatch

5.

Then foul macadam
blossomed like rosemary
in the old tapestry
where unicorns deigned
to weave a fantasy
truer I swear than

6.

Judge Mace his black
shroud his skeletal
body & soul
whose veins decant
vapors to turn the
innocent eye
dry as the dead.

When a United States judge sentenced two of the pacifists to six years in Federal prison . . . he clearly ignored sound discretion. The powers of the bench include the power to fix sentences on those found guilty, but they do not include the right to impose punishment out of all proportion to the crime.

—The New York *Times*

7.

Indicted
charged with creating
children   confusion
legerdemain   flowers
felonious picnics.
Jews in Babylon
we sit and mourn
somewhere in Mace's
mad eyes' space

> "I have tried all the conventional and legal forms of protest to little or no avail," says Philip, who argues that both Christ and Paul allowed the possibility of civil disobedience when man's law counters God's."
>
> —*Time*

8.

TO PHILIP

Compassionate, casual as a good face
(a good heart goes without saying)
someone seen in the street; or
infinitely rare, once, twice in a lifetime

that conjunction we call brother or friend.
Biology, mythology cast up clues.
We grew together, stars made men
by cold design; instructed

sternly (no variance, not by a hair's
breadth) in course and recourse. In the heavens
in our mother's body, by moon and month
were whole men made.
We obeyed then, and were born.

OBIT

We die

showing like frayed pockets, space within
without, for loss.
                    Pain in eyes, a ragged
animal before the gun;
                    muzzily—
can death do any harm
life hasn't done? maybe
(dreamily) *death*
turns old dogs
into fish hillsides butterflies
teaches a new
trick or two

THIS CRUCIFIX

Where great love is
are miracles, the saints say
who are held
in principle, to no proof.

No
its man
clings there, life's last straw
death's
crude analogate.

Cold man
we push the gospel
at a dead heart.

No proof. Day after day I turn
to cry the healer for some hint.
From dying eyes
there flies

a sliver cock
to taste the bitter air

foul foul.
and someday—*fair*?

THE CLOCK IN THE SQUARE REMINDS ME OF CERTAIN LIVES

Ineffectuals
chained, reined to time's beaten track—
simulacra all, strangers to action, passion

strike the hour, lurch away
pale as linen
the pharaohs of long refusal.

THERE MUST BE A GOD

I thought I heard
my own life say it
and the crumbling streets
and alkys mumbling, and the shot landscape
of my youth; *gone—*
trees, sweetness, euphoria

Yet in hair or hand
a rose, blown, ragged,
a victory somewhere
like a torch in the hands of a runner
beat, dying, but on his feet.

Let there be a God!
is man's big news;
let Him show as much heart
as goodness musters;

leave us alone
to make do, fumble about, fret through;
He must leave us our sins
to learn and ravel;
sweat, start false, feint, dissimulate.

Let Him be a dying vine, a back door
marked "colored only"
day old bread, wino's wine.
Let Him "stand with the fate
of the majority"
A shepherd, if he likes folklore,
like the Roman gypsies
at Christmas time
blowing their big sheep bladders
like an ass's brag
crying, not Christmas
but their own sores snd rags.

O incarnation is a hard word.
There is some flesh I could not take.
On my way to a Bowery wedding
the Bowery sty;
in a Bellevue ward
sour lees, sour wine;
uptown east, spiffy aseptic dogs
parading cloud nine;
the doormen's preternatural fishy stare—

ah wilderness! He marvels
I am more astonished
with what I find here
than with what I bring!

SOME SORT OF EXPLANATION, BETTER THAN NONE

I cultivate a grin
that takes into account

a rear end
bruised
by an ass's iron shoe

Meantime
that knock you hear
is death's drumstick
tapping his forehead 3 times
with the knowing look
of woody woodpecker;

for this, and other
prudential courtesies
  of wind & weather
  of lack and luck
  of the fair fall
  of bones them bones—

love life!

COME ALIVE
(on the Long Island Railroad)

I had lost everything for a year
a stick in a blind hand—
conundrums, fantasy

the blind hand struck, the stick
stuck rotting in rich ground.
Four seasons come and gone.

Imagine a face? summon
sustenance, vision, up from that ground?

My mind took no fire
from fiery truth; my hands hung
like hanged necks, dead, dead as a show.

But the children of Birmingham
clairvoyant, compassionate among the dead—

I see you all night long.
Dawn winds freshen. The cock
makes children by the clock.
The trees lift up their dawn.

SOMEWHERE THE EQUATION BREAKS DOWN

between the perfect
(invisible, Plato said)
and the imperfect
that comes at you on the street,
stench and cloth and fried eyes;
between the wired bones of the dead
stuttering, shamed
and the marvelous lucid spirit
that moves in the body's spaces
a rainbow fish bebind glass—
decide. O coincide!

NOVEMBER 20, 1965

Subway faces beheaded
in the blade of your eyes.
Life? step in, be
lost.
All heaven's bells
nod in accord
like Bottlcelli curls;
yes O yes

I think of my father and mother;
their dignity measures

the horror—
that leap
marked like a third rail's
mortal sputter;
danger!

They leapt, and live,
the stranger's wounds succored
the lost child safe in arms.

PEACEMAKING IS HARD
(Jim and Sally)

hard almost as war.
The difference being one
we can stake life upon
and limb and thought and love.

I stake this poem out
dead man to a dead stick
to tempt an Easter chance—
if faith may be
truth, our evil chance
penultimate at last

not last. We are not lost.

When these lines gathered
of no resource at all
serenity and strength,
it dawned on me—

a man stood on his nails

as ash like dew, a sweat
smelling of death and life.
Our evil Friday fled,

the blind face gently turned
another way, toward life

a man walks in his shroud

SEMINAR

One speaker
an impeccable
Californian
impelled to explain

The Chinese Belong In China
The Russians In Russia.
we however—
messiah oversoul
a pink   muscled clear-eyed
Texan dream
fumigating
Hanoi privies
from above—
napalm   jigger bombs gas
God's saniflush, in sum—

The gentleman was
four square as State
or the pentateuch;
sans beard, rope sandals, foul talk, pot—
a fire extinguisher
on Pentecost day;
exuding good will
like a mortician's convention
in a plague year.

Indeed yes.
There is nothing sick
(the corpse said)

about death
Come in.

1967—VIETNAM

Two hands (fixation, horror)
raised in the stone doorway
falter, let drop
wine and fire from the empty cup.

You avail—nothing.

Something? tell
the bread that failed, the circuses that fell

A CIVIL RIGHTS DEMONSTRATION

That morning I weighed
like a Dickens brat
no expectations. Would I march
capped in bells like Christ's fool or Christ?

who walked with us
borne on what wind?
driven Jews, sere in vein and eye?
Sharpeville's seventy, brave in red ribbons?

O who will turn
dust to a man on march?I taste in mouth
the dust of Jews, the *durst not kill* of prophets
a taste that kills.

Bread loaf king
shelved, mouldering; a churchmice clergy start

cut, flee for cover. See how they run
like field mice under the teeth or scythe. Like men.

BERGAMO: Instructions for Going Forth

(News item:
In a fresh dug crypt
under the new seminary,
they are constructing
a 2,000 seat church
against the day
when John XXIII of Bergamo
is declared saint.)

Alas death's
toss bones
like unlucky dice
among medicine men
hawkers spivs

might he not
cast a more thoughtful eye
on other
exits, intercessions?

Birds of paradise
long distance runners
acrobats wandering clerks

invitations dawns
catherine wheels
love poetry death by fire

sandal wood pyres ashes
borne upon streams
from the heartland
a land (at last) of no
morticians

DIARY (Easter, 1966)

I hadn't walked the tow path in Central Park
for six months, having flapped southward

like a lame duck under circumstances
that yield here to self-censoring.

I left; the Park gave scarcely a shrug,
the big body
autumnal, luxuriant,
a vague disinterest in eye
a hung up blear of smog
a rare fitful candor, a dog's
intelligence, an old horse's look. O sun!

Absent, the Park was in my heart
not noble, remorseful, remembering;
a wink, a New York shrug.
Nevertheless, went with me
an animal shadow, all its animals—
seals, weeping
the absurdest tears of all creation—

I called good night
that last time, November 20. The sea lion
a shmoo's dream of beatitude, a feast afloat
turned on me
his rheumy uncle's eye;
time for all that   time
to envy eagles, clouds like slow birds,
gulls slow as paper from the huffing stacks
time for return. He'd see me.

Southward, I thought of paeons to the Park.
Rio children had a park in mind
mud pies, dust cake, the hominoids like children.
Alas, their bones scrawled in the dust
alas, and the winds took the word away, as years
our bones

Home again, I visit the seal;
his majesty, cold in his ingrown mask
tight in his poorhouse trousers,

promulgates
the good life, laissez-faire,
49 brands of fish.

Ponderous
half in, half out of the water
his leather flipper
tapping the sea wall like God the Father
or Teddy Roosevelt
WELCOMES ME, NAME OF ALL!

O the Park descends on the city
like a celestial napkin, as if heaven
were all of earth, the fusty smell
of animals in arks, of cornered lives and deaths.
What is our freedom, Peter?
Obedience.
You have answered well;

I give you—exodus.
Wandering Jew
you have a Jew for God.
The Park
unreal as real estate
under the flood
bears you away, ashore:
The city!

SALVATION HISTORY

I had a nightmare—
the rickety shack brought down
I was sheltering in;
from sleep to death
gone, all coped in dream

What then? I had never lived?
it well might be.

Without friends, what am I?
their noon and moon, my own
Without friends—what?
dead, unborn, my light
quenched, never struck.

The piteous alternatives
life simulates!
streets haunt, faces hang

but I mark
like an unquenched man
merciful interventions

a clean end or beginning
someone to die for   some love to sing

WEST SIDE STORY

A Broadway hash joint, a Puerto Rican
short orders *2 burgers with cheese,*
2 without; *onions, ketchup*

in 4 minutes flat with style, verve, and
a rare smile in a sour borough.

Far from Gracie Mansion and the gentle Sheep
Meadow. He hasn't smelled roses in years

but he wears them. While
nightmares hustle like rats
a night's undoing
                    he feeds modestly
(a few inferior loaves, a few
greasy fish) the city's poor.
Winner? we have no other.
In a bad time, blessed are you , for blessing me.

AND WHAT ARE WE?

Not like the rich
a fist of worms for a heart;
nor like the poor
consumed with making do,
rancor at dawn, futility at dusk

say; like a slum child
in a filthy yard—
a spool, a few crossed sticks

something different from himself—
the doll wound on a bobbin
almost talks back,
almost stalks away.

Was this the way He meant us?
meddlesome
proud, not docile

to stand to Him, thwart, amaze Him still!

FACING IT

Who could declare your death,
obedient as Stylites, empty as death's head
majestic as the world's sun   moving
into night?

It was a hollow death; we
dread it like a plague. Thieves die this way,
charlatans, rejects. A good man's thought recoils;

to grow old yes,
home and faces
drifting out of mind. Abrupt violence yes
a quick mercy on disease

but not, not this; the mother's face
knotted, mottled with horror,

time's cruel harrowing
furies at the reins of fortune
wild horses dragging
the heroic dishonored body on time's ground.

O for an act of God! we cry, before death utterly
reduce to dust
        that countenance, that grace and beauty.

But
come wild hope, to dead end. War, murder,
anguish, fratricide.

No recourse. The case of Jesus Christ
is closed. Make what you will

desire, regret, he lies
stigmatized, a broken God
the world had sport of.

Risen? we have not turned that page.

THE CHURCH IS NAMED MOTHER OF FAIR LOVE

Panic of dark minds sounds
about the level brows, the austere skull
that harbors like a shell
the inmost mystery of all years.
Sterness, compassion in those eyes;

come near, the quick and dead Be born of me.

HELP ME SOMEONE

I should like to know please
the name of that girl
lauded in some obscure corner
of the press

dead in Paris
buried in Père Lachaise cemetery,
dedicated it was said, to the common good

an American girl
solicitous
succoring
showing the city of light
an unaccustomed
incandescence.

Where then?
her bones make
so small a sound
in the noiseless sockets
of history

and *learn! learn!* is the law
whereby we stand
and they
cut free.

SAINT FRANCIS

Sometimes
I come through
like the first note
of a trumpet
fired with morning
round as a Saturn ring

hot and cold
as a virgin's brow

highest C

off your radar your purported
ears
stuffed like mouths
with yesterday's omelettes
trussed like turkeys
groaning;
they have stolen
alas my
heart my
gizzard my
2 rare
unstrung pearls.

No; there went ME;
my heart's thrum thrum my
gizzard's auld lang syne my
pearls' sound of milk
warm from the tit, hitting
(squall) the cat's eyeball

unheard unheard as love
mostly on
Thanksgiving Christmas your
trussed capons your
burning babes.

No—
the sweet spontaneous
animals hear
me and
fear not and
draw
near.

7. Night Flight to Hanoi

The following twelve poems were written on the spot, in the course of a trip to Hanoi, January 31–February 18, 1968.

PRAYER

I left Cornell
with half a wit; six mismated socks
ski underwear, a toothbrush,
passport, one hundred good
green dollars, their faces
virtuous as ancestors,
the chamois sack
Karl Meyer gave me years ago, handmade
by dispossessed Georgia Negroes.

Later, dismay; no Testament.
I must construct out of oddments, abrasions,
vapor trails, dust, pedicabs
three crosshatch continents, Brooks Brothers embassies
their male models dressed to kill—

all He meant and means. I touch
shrapnel and flesh, and risk my reason
for the truth's sake, an ignorant hung head.

Man of one book, stand me in stead.

NIGHT FLIGHT TO HANOI

In a bar in Vientiane
they said to us
like Job's mockers;
thanks to your own ever loving bombers
you may never see
the northern lights, Hanoi.

Then, by bat radar
we crawled that corridor
blind as bats,
a wing and a prayer.

Came in!
the big glare of a klieg eye
held us, hooked, death's open season.
We held breath, fish
baited, not landed.

Ended; the pale faces of flowers
said suddenly, out of season
something than death other, unuttered.

Exiles we went in
safe kept, cherished by strangers.

BOMBARDMENT

Like those who go aground
willfully, knowing our human
absurd estate can but be bettered
in the battering hands of the gods—

yet mourning traitorously the sun and moon
and one other face, and heat of hearth—

went under
like a blown match. The gases flare on the world's combustible
flesh.

CHILDREN IN THE SHELTER

Imagine; three of them.

As though survival
were a rat's word,

and a rat's death
waited there at the end

and I must have
in the century's boneyard
heft of flesh and bone in my anns

I picked up the littlest
a boy, his face
breaded with rice (his sister calmly feeding him
as we climbed down)

In my arms fathered
in a moment's grace, the messiah
of all my tears. I bore, reborn

a Hiroshima child from hell.

FLOWERS

A flower is single jeopardy—
only one death; matrons' scissors, dogs'
natural deflowering; choose! Meantime
dare time and wind and war. Be

no one's metronome, discount
in a lover's hand, the ways
we die—routine, wrong analogy.

I start these words because
a girl on a bicycle
swaying

bears a few flowers
homeward through war, a double jeopardy.
I held
breath for her, her flowers, on the wheel of fire,
the world, no other.

Sentries, we passed, no countersign

except *good-bye*
forced first last word of all.

SONG

The maids sing at their scrubbing
the cooks at the stove—

shame, women, such lightness of mind
ill becomes; think rather on
Death   Judgment   Heaven   Hell

the names of the bombers
that bear in their skull
your names, memorized in fire.

THE PILOTS, RELEASED

1.

When I think of you it is always (forgive me)
of disposable art; 50 designs, the damp woodcut
of 50 States, the physiognomy of camp—

Innocence (mom), *pietas* (pop), the household gods
guarding the gates guarded by you, O proxies
for all providence   Saigon to

Rio to Congo   your chilling logic
draws blood   a blood bank   a blank bloody
check drawn on the living
                                        who thereupon
        here   there   and tomorrow by all accounts
                are dead

2.

The trouble with innocence
is itself, itself in the world—
the GI who had a wife
but never imagined one
had children true to form
whose lives described
like dance or geometry
the outer edge, drawn there
in diametric blood—
thus far love, and no further.

MY NAME

If I were Pablo Neruda
or William Blake
I could bear, and be eloquent

an American name in the world
where men perish
in our two murderous hands

Alas Berrigan
you must open those hands
and see, stigmatized in their palms,
the broken faces
you yearn toward

you cannot offer
being powerless as a woman
under the rain of fire—
life, the cover of your body.

Only the innocent die.
Take up, take up
the bloody map of the century.
The long trek homeward begins
into the land of unknowing.

8. Trial Poems

1. WINGS

We flew in for trial
a butterfly came to rest on our big
Boeing wing
pulsed there, a hand in ballet motion, a heartbeat.
I wished the little tacker luck. He was
technologically innocent, flying
by grace of the US Air Control Command
because his wing-spread
(I checked this)
lay somewhere below the danger area
of the breadth
of minor aircraft.

2. THE MARSHAL

The marshal is taking my measure
snip snip snip, crossways, back and front
he X's me, society's darling, dun shirt and pants.
He grins past my shoulder
a clown head at odds with its fate.

His ribald revolver eye
(steel sights, barrel nose)
is taking my measure.
I will wear khaki (he grins) and love it
for years and years
and play
night and day
cops and robbers;
in dreams, for years
will scramble the wall like a spider,
fall
piecemeal,
into my savior's throttling arms.

3. JOHN UREY

In our big cruel cell block
designed like a city hospital
for the spreading of disease
I came on an old pulp sheet;
in a corner
of its rubbishy mind
the news shone, a priest who made history.
John Urey
in the Manhattan sty Dickens slogged
one hundred years after
(preserved to this day; slums being
our manifest destiny)
    'dens where dogs would howl to lie
    ruined houses open to the street—
    hideous tenements
                                their names
    drawn from robbery and murder;
                                                    whatever is
    loathsome, drooping and decayed . . .'
The priest, in and out of an alehouse
ministered to slaves by night,
sought like a slave by the carnivore
founding fathers
                        whose dentures gleam
in the old portraits, like sharks
in grand banks of privilege.

The night before our trial
opens its jaws (an old shark yawn, gold-capped
with privilege, boredom, bankruptcy),
I think of John Urey;
down the bleak corridor
Philip's typewriter,
                        the stick of a blind prophet
argues the deities blind,
Tom Lewis ponders tomorrow—

from swine tending at Lewisburg prison
to Baltimore court, one scene and the same;
the parable of Jesus
keeps sane his gentle spirit. . . .

Wherefore John Urey, make common cause with us
indicted felons, for pouring of blood and fire
on murderous licenses;
lead into court
                              the great society's
everyday catch;
                              the dying children, burned, blinded
in Washington rose gardens;
give evidence upon that power
wasted like seed or life's blood
on whoring and butchery.

John Urey, tell our Father
face to face, in beatific vision
we hallowed hold His name.

4. GUILTY

Supersonic time
that noses the ether
like a hell hound
on mercy and bombing missions
bore me here
dropped me like a dud

I sit in the town stocks
for ten thousand years
a judge's or butcher's scrawl
GUILTY around my neck.

On a park bench in Japan
a man's shadow sits
after the bomb's wink
ten thousand years

until God wink again
like a lucky fisherman
and a man's mouth snap
shut   on the hook they say
God says stands for hope

The man screams or yawns
unheard from as s fish
or a man at rope's end
by Goya or Daumier

5. A TYPICAL DAY IN THE MUNICIPAL ZOO

We sit, we walk our cage
day after day;
at night, the moon
striped like a tiger
leaps on us with a cry.

Unlikely men, white, black
sweating with rage and grief
our diet decreed
by our own prophetic guts—

the prison poems of Ho,
the sayings of Chairman Jesus.

6. EUCHARIST

7 a.m. trial day,
courtesy of Warden Foster,
the San Jose vineyards
and a common baking shop

we took
in a workman's cracked cup
at a slum table

prisoners' pot luck

7. THE BOXES OF PAPER ASH

the size of infant caskets
were rolled in on a dolly
heaped there like cordwood
or children after a usual
air strike on Hanoi.
I heard between heartbeats
of Jesus and his hangman
the children's mouths mewing
for the breasts of murdered women
the blackened hands beating
the box of death for breath.

8. THE VERDICT

Everything before was a great lie.
Illusion, distemper, the judge's eye
Negro and Jew for rigorists,
spontaneous vengeance. The children die
singing in the furnace. They say in hell
heaven is a great lie.
Years, years ago
my mother moves in youth. In her
I move too, to birth, to youth, to this.
The judge's *toc toc* is time's steel hand
summoning; *come priest from the priest hole. Risk!*
Everything else
is a great lie. Four walls, home, love, youth
truth untried, all, all is a great lie.
The truth the judge shuts in his two eyes.

Come Jesuit, the university cannot
no nor the universe, nor vatic Jesus
imagine. Imagine! Everything before
was a great lie.
                    Philip, your freedom
stature, simplicity, the ghetto where the children
malinger, die—
                    Judge Thomsen
strike, strike with a hot hammer
the hour, the truth. The truth has birth
all former truth must die. Everything
before; all faith and hope, and love itself
was a great lie.

9. Cornell Poems

ARRIVAL (1967)

Left New York by Mohawk jet
        for Ithaca;
        fair trading of cities? no.
    but recalled during that flight
Pascal; *the heart has its reasons.*

    Yes. That organ
        of inmost sight and surprise
    imperated, and I came

a minor
    humorously welcomed
        species in the great think tank
    me

whom even
    crowned with his crown
        the incumbent whale
    -'s regnant eye rolls
                sidewise to see

IN EXALTATION OF SO SIMPLE A THING, AN AUTUMN TREE

Has not let blood
nor lied in his teeth
nor made mock
nor defrauded
nor worshipped idols
nor extinguished truth

But
like anemone
or a golden fish—
blushes, pales at the nearing
bridegroom

whom you (we)
in fear-ridden
vocables
flee
crying

reality!

AUTUMN, THE STREAMS ARE HEAVY

One day; coming home
treading effortfully
(the gorges, a geography, a friendship
the years make difficult
terrain)

sudden
air water
conjoin
I am immersed, you
shaped heaven and earth
I am nowhere safe
like a bloodlet Christ
taken
hapless in my crown
my murder,
Father.

Was, no not one
sweet reason
why we should not
like fish mouths
drink the light and
die
like fish in Christian legend,
rise
pied like rainbows from the cave

No reason!
trees and fish
whisper like elders;
seek
in breaking bones the hero's springing,
in self sacrifice
the breathing span
of bridges and new men—
in night watches and sweat
the icy lakes
death may not sour or slake!

TO A SOLDIER, SLEEPING IN AN AIRPORT WAITING ROOM

(after the Pentagon)

I prayed as I went past—
his thought might flow
gentle as water, lax from his hands
languishing in no
five-sided hell,
the labyrinthe
we sat in
like clubbed watch dogs
two weeks before.

No D.C. nightmare, soldier.
O that the sleep
were wakening, the innocent inwardness
yours for good!
wasps from a hive
the troops poured out, a seventh plague
from the porticoes. Sleep on—
take oath to sleep, the Pentagon
doth murder sleep! under the brute flares
they hustled us, harmless as flies
into the spider's parlor.

Dreams strip you
like a bride's handmaids
of filth of office,
hire you out
to no one's whoring power. Your body's
fratricidal steel
plunge like a lover's tool into the fire
where lust forgets its fury,
the plowshares
like Sunday dolphins play
earth, sea,
for all their worth and birth.

DEATH OF A DEER

Impaled
in big mindless lights
he touched heels to us
as a drumming stick its head

then arched away
folding his legs
like the elbows of a drummer
pausing—
a split second late!
we broke that beat, that heart—
threw him
headlong into tbe shark jaws
of a hurtling Buick

he lay
bloody as birth, the wet head
just born
            beyond—
nostrils, eyes, mouth
roped with blood, the tragic essence
of our air, when the innocent
breathe, and bleed for it

It was war time, our Volkswagen
thin as eggshell; we stood there
he died there, trailing
the fouled life line; guts
genitals, spreadeagled.
the unanswerable eyes
of a murdered child, the dun
peasant rags
night flares

and cold as ikons or iconoclasts, the
savage sophisticated gods,
our fun done
                    helpless
as the dead
to resurrect

THE SERMON ON THE MOUNT, AND THE WAR THAT WILL NOT END FOREVER

Jesus came down from Crough Patrick
crazy with cold, starry with vision.
The sun undid what the moon did; unlocked him.

Light headed ecstasy; *love*
he commended, as tongue and teeth
fixed on it; *love* for meat after fast;

then *poverty*, &
mild and clean hearts stood commended.

Next spring, mounted Crough Patrick
and perished.
The word came down
comes down and down, comes what he said

men say, gainsay, say nay.

Not easy for those who man
the mountain, forever ringed and fired.
And the children, the children
                                                            die
die like our last chance
                                               day
                                                      after Christian day

10. The Dark Night of Resistance

CERTAIN OCCULT UTTERANCES FROM THE UNDER GROUND AND ITS GUARDIAN SPHINX

If you seek pleasure in everything
you must seek pleasure in nothing

if you wish to possess everything
you must desire to possess nothing

if you wish to become all
you must desire to be nothing

if you wish to know all
you must desire to know nothing

if you wish to arrive where you know not
you must go by a way you know not

if you wish to possess what you do not
you must dispossess

if you wish to become new
you must become as dead

A PENNY PRIMER IN THE ART OF FORGETFULNESS

What is the price of the future?
Forgetting the future

What is the price of revolution?
Forgetting the revolution

What things are to be forgotten?
The good things

Only?
Also the evil things

All things?
All things

What good things for instance?
Father   mother   family   friends

also books   tastes   a settled abode
the view at the window
ecstasy   flowers
the turn and tide of season

What bad things?
Offenses   hurts   foolishness   also
instinctive lunges   settled enmities
termites   rank offenses   shark mouths
the stuttering etc of nightmare

What is the value of this?
Connection

Where will it lead?
Forget where it will lead

You ask me to become a boor
an aardvark an amputee?
No. A Human.

How a human?
A human is one enabled
to forget
both method and way
            consumed

in the act & grace of the human
the entire gift

What gift act grace?
We must borrow
one outlawed debased word—
love

And then?
Then then then

Run off   empty your mind
like a dawn slops
or I shall I swear
by the Zen fathers
thwack your dense shoulders
with this bamboo

11. America Is Hard to Find

AMERICA IS HARD TO FIND

Hard to find;
wild strawberries swans herons deer
those things we long to be
metamorphosed in and out of our sweet sour skins—
good news housing Herefords holiness
wholeness
Hard to find; free form men and women
harps hope food mandalas meditation
Hard to find; lost not found rare as radium rent free
uncontrollable uncanny a chorus
Jesus Buddha Moses founding fathers horizons
hope (in hiding)
Hard to find; America
now if America is doing wel1 you may expect Vietnamese to do well if power is virtuous the powerless will not be marked for death if the heart of man is flourishing so will plants and wild animals (But alas alas so also vice versa)
Hard to find. Good bread is hard to find. Of course. The hands are wielding swords The wild animals fade out like Alice's cat's smile Americans are hard to find The defenseless fade away like hundred year pensioners The sour faced gorgons remain. . . .
But listen brothers and sisters this disk floats downward a flying saucer in the macadam back yard where one paradise tree a hardy weed sends up its signal flare (spring!)
fly it! turn it on! become
hard to find become be born
out of the sea Atlantis out in the wilds America
This disk like manna miraculous loaves and fishes
exists to be multiplied savored shared
play it! learn it! have it by heart!
Hard to find! where the frogs boom boom in the spring twilight
search for the odor of good bread follow it
man man is near (though hard to find)
a rib cage growing red wild as strawberries a heart!
imagine intelligence imagine peaceable caressing food planting music

making
hands Imagine Come in!
P.S. Dear friends I choose to be a jail bird (one species is flourishing) in a kingdom of fowlers
Like strawberries good bread
swans herons Great Lakes I shall shortly be
hard to find
an exotic uneasy inmate of the NATIONALLY ENDOWED ELECTRONICALLY INESCAPABLE ZOO
remember me I am
free at large untamable not nearly
as hard to find as America

QUESTION AND ANSWER

Query: Shall a man then return
to the womb of his mother, reborn?
Jesus: As you said: earth, old basket-born, hard-beaked hen
wants you for egg.
No, I hereby (he scrawled on the inside of his shell)
attest to my first
Will and Testament.
I shall go forth bare-assed as a new moon,
stellar as baby Jesus.
Everyone's sight and scandal. Yes and No.
And the vast milky way perhaps between.

I WILL SIGN MY NAME

Now what the hell sort of dog's life is left to limp?
I may not mean what I see.
The FBI has devised for this emergency a poetry censor
whose eyes flame like an alcoholic's,
smoke like Beelzebub's dry ice or dry armpit

when the bubonic smel1 of a poetic name-place
falls under its snub snout.
I may not name river.
No, nor mountain, street, alley nor valley.
At least I will sign my name.
Now hold your nose, eyes, ears,
in a one-mile perimeter of infernal headquarters.
All hell will shortly like dull scissors and sirens
gouge, saw, at the inner ear.
Ready? Set? Then.
Daniel Berrigan.

12. Prison Poems

TULIPS IN THE PRISON YARD

Many poets, believe me, could do better by your
sovereign beauty, your altogether subtle
transfiguration of blank nature—
so winds, nights, sunlight
colorless wraiths, are drawn into
what can only be called a "new game."
Well. I will not glory
in infirmity. Yeats, Wordsworth would look once
breathe deeply, sharpen their quills,
with a flourish pluck you from time.
But.
You are jail-yard blooms, you wear bravery with a difference.
You are born here will die here;
making you, by excess of suffering
and transfiguration of suffering, ours.

I see prisoners pass
in the dead spur of spring, before you show face

Are you their glancing tears
the faces of wives and children, the yin yang of hearts
to fro like hanged necks
perpetual cruelty, absurdity?

The prisoners
pass and pass; shades of men, pre-men,
khaki ghosts, shame, futility.
Between smiles, between reason for smiles, between
life as fool's pace and life as celebrant's flame—
aeons.
Yet, thank you. Against the whips
of ignorant furies, the slavish pieties of judas priests
you stand, a first flicker in the brain's soil, the precursor
of judgment.
Dawn might be, man may be

or
spelling it out in the hand's palm
of a blind mute

God is fire, is love.

PATIENCE, HARD VIRTUE

Patience, tedious non Virtue
hangs around hangs around
Pantheon, cave of Aeolus
the last hour of Socrates
wherever the action is—
near hero, or near beer or
money laid on the slow horse
History, out of Time
(fool and money soon parted.)

He's waiting.   Outlasting
poverty programs, pogroms,
skins and their trade.
Hangs around.   Hangers-on sidle up
to stand beside.
Dumb animals, still
or addled streams, straw,
stars, flowers that
transmogrify the show—

It seems to me when the Man
makes meat of us or less
the less is still the more;
the meat is greater heart;
cut to the bone, patience
outlasts the butcher's tool.

Hard, hard, no resolution:
the con's infernal whine,
the druggie's addled tongue,

intemperance, cowardice,
the monstrous world's mirror
held up to nature, held
corrective, cruel, exact
to our own face, day
after night, imposed
night upon sorrowing day.

The universe waits on us;
great patience on a lesser.
A prisoner's days run,
the weeks a slow drawn pain,
the years standing like stone.
Great nature doing time.
Hard time, easy time—
clobbering or tender hands
jack boots or juggernauts

"Consider the lilies—"
good news, good humor, grace.
I had rather so live, a few
brothers assailed, than mick-mock
whoring Caesar's strut.

Who pays, who renounces, who
makes that news anew?
unheard of news, heard now
seen now, touched now. I had rather—
but how descry it? My eyes
flare like a lamp in rain—

Hang around. Patience. Hear it:
The children live, the children
rise from My Lai ditch.

A PRAYER TO THE BLESSED TRINITY

I'm locked into the sins of General Motors
My guts are in revolt at the culinary equivocations of
General Foods

Hang over me like an evil shekinah, the missiles of
General Electric.
Now we shall go from the Generals to the Particulars.
Father, Son, Holy Ghost
Let me shake your right hands in the above mentioned order
Unmoved Motor, Food For Thought, Electric One.
I like you better than your earthly idols.
You seem honest and clear-minded and reasonably resolved
To make good on your promise.
Please: owe it to yourselves not less than to us,
Warn your people: beware of adulterations.

IN PRISON, AS OUT, TIME IS OF THE ESSENCE

Methodical rampage
Texans, conquistadors, empire builders!
No, teach my eyes to rejoice
in 1 sugaring unbudded tree, 1 star
framed in a barred window, broad existence
narrowed to a keeper's eye. Gandhi and Jesus
in time of prevarication, my teachers of honor.
Grow small, embrace in 2 arms, time grown small
the *nada* of hermits and the friends of God.

ALMOST EVERYBODY IS DYING HERE: ONLY A FEW ACTUALLY MAKE IT

at 12:30 sharp
as though to underscore
some unassuageable grief
a man's head fell to one side
in the prison hospital.
No record of heart disease
a morning's weakness only. His neck went limp

in the pale March sunlight
like a wax man's.
his hands opened, a beggar's hesitant reach
before a rich man's shadow.
Near, there and
gone.

O DANBURY, TO WHAT SHALL I COMPARE THEE?

Like coming up against testy Charon in a bad time
—or New York customs, en route from Hanoi, '68.
Notes stuffed in a paper bag.
Resolved: they'll have my life before
they have those words, scrawled in shelters
under their besotted bombs.

Some moments you're willing to die for,
die rather than have undone . . .
I scrawl this, lights out, at a barred window.
Snow filigrees the April green.
Before they lay their cotton-picking paws on them
I'll eat these notes
alphabetize with good news
my prophetic guts.

WE WERE PERMITTED TO MEET TOGETHER IN PRISON TO PREPARE FOR TRIAL

yesterday, the usual stiff-necked shakedown
room possessions person—then
entered the seemly company,
fellow indicted and co-conspirators.
nuns, priests, friends
the inadmissible evidence of their lives

vivid as flowers in a dustbin
(the big eye outside, the praying mantis),
word went around quietly; we have bread and wine!
that unwinking eye
glassing over with boredom
the mice in all seriousness played
the Jesus game. a reading from Ezekiel
on the doomed city. Silence. Philip whispering over the bread
(a con, a magian), over the 'mt. dew' tin can.
we broke and passed the loaf, the furtive hands
of endangered animals.
my body given for you. my blood outpoured.
indictable action! as in the first instance
of vagrant Jesus, in whose flesh rumors and truth
collided; usual penalty, rigorously applied.

My friends, it is the savor of life
you passed to me; vines, the diminished loaf
lost hillsides where the sun
sets the grapes beating like a hive
of human hearts; Cornell gorges, the distant sea
Block Island swung like a hammock from its moorings -
I come to myself
a beast in a shoe box
Sport
of the king of the cats

A TYPICAL 6:00 P.M. IN THE FUN HOUSE

He yelled *count finished!* The machinery
swings back on its demented elbow. We are stars or cattle
or the 16 winds or nest eggs or Fort Knox or quintuplets.
Some days my brain burns
a loaded circuit, with the massed burden of it all,
the bad news funneled into the dark tunnel
a raging train, a stinking herd—

7 layers of Sodom on the spirit.
Other days I make it,
counting like prayer beads, the hours dropped or palmed.
A lotus sprouts in the privy's filth.
The small tree outside, unfit for a man's dead weight, breathes.
hang on!

YOU COULD MAKE A SONG OF IT A DIRGE OF IT A HEARTBREAKER OF IT

EVERYONE everyone in america
carries the war around with him
N. Mailer carries the war with him
2 inches on his waste line
B. Graham carries the war with him
at the root of his tongue   where the tongue forks out
left; turning a bible page
right; tasting the apples in the W. House garden
Bobby Seale carries the war with him
shackles to shoe laces.
The dying man in the cancer ward carries the war—
face to wall, kicked off the skids of the medicos.
The break-&-entry man   the acid freaks   the boy & girl
carry the war with them   Making love
is mortal sin   the warmakers march
the lovemakers die
Cardinals carry the war around, a sign of the double-cross
Jews carry the war   the yarmulke sits
on the classified head of Kissinger
The kids
toss a switchblade in the spring mud—
Territory!   they cry
carving the breathing earth like a turkey corpse.

8 O'CLOCK MORNING SCENE

a crowded car-load
of expertise

disgorges each A.M.
in the compound

running like beetles
each 2 his bureau

briefcases bulging
foreheads furrowed

mockups   motivations
instruments   lobotomies

up pills   down pills
blueprints   fingerprints

funny funny
a sparrow stretches

a wing   a leg   yawns
in the dawn light

nothing ever happens
here

DECEMBER 2, 1971

One of them, a benign corrupt cop
with the face of a bishop's crook
locks me in, jocund at midnight.

Goose pimples, recognition
an Auschwitz moment
as if a renegade jew
ushered his rabbi, with a flourish, a persuasive
push
into
"our best yes sir absolutely Grade A reserved oven."

FOR PHILIP'S BIRTHDAY

October '71

1.

Praise God I say yes
Even for deprivations!
Starved in nostril and eye
we make do, make do
With near stocks and stones,
Flat approximations
of the squamous and famous real things
Which if I could I would
Make come true for you
Like godmother or god.

But knowing how justice burns
In a brother's fingertips
Knowing nothing is won
Neither will, passion, sustenance,
Freedom or freedom's outreach
Until all, all are fed—
And standing somewhat this side
Of almighty wheel and deal—
What can I make for you?
Simulacra, images,
cosmic complicity
with all that lives and moves
On earth's majestical
Land mass and waterfall.

3.

Because we remember, it is possible to dismember
The demon haunted will. Why we are here.
A thighbone
Wreathed with its laurel flesh, walks on and on
Toward the promise.
Because we remember our Father
It is possible to be sons. Because we remember

Our brothers, it is possible
To bind up wounds we never dealt.
Possible.
Unbungled, courageous, birth and 2nd birth
—new phases,
Genetic transfigurations.
The thighbone
One, alive, remembering, incandescent, soul. Toward.

4.

The reason we are in prison encompasses
The harmonies of nature; visible, invisible, beneficent.
Plunging one's wrists
Into the sources and springs of being
So cold they scald,
Lifting eyes to the dispassionate heavens
So distant they blind.
We wear like a flower our reason; it endures.
We compose our reason, a prayer; God bends to it.
O place us in the very tic and mortal danger
Of self renewing choice, the heart riding its high wire!
We are here neatly as crystals telling time.
A nest of woven thorns, swans' down,
haven of the warm unborn,
desert and arctic temperatures; survival.
More; the grace that renders gracious.
O delighting Spirit, we are here; grant space.

5.

In a bad time good religion? Rare, so rare,
Like wild strawberries or thyme in factory
Slag, hardly ever.
Wherever growth; rank, outrageous.

Jesus freaks, born with a 3rd throttling
Hand, contemplators drowned like drunken
Sailors in the sap of their navel, actionists
bloodying the ape in the mirror

That beats them bloody, a bloody bore.
Religion?   At the edges it were better to keep silence.

6.

What finally to hope for?   something enduring
might come of simple endurance, a cheerful mien,
sight of moon and stars, faces
that mirror across the void, our faces.
Harsh, hardly victory.
Logic. The text of the years leads to this place.

Make then, like a Greek ecstatic, virtue of necessity.

7.

With us it was never
winner and loser
but you, a big AND,
and I and our two hands.
Who cared if overhead
napkined and beaked
in the air a buzzard stink
in the air the wrong gods!
heel to heel, we ran.
Both
made it, death to life.
So no hindmost and no
devil to take either.

MY FATHER

1.

All bets were on; he was dying
back in '62; found by mother 2:00 a.m.
on the john floor, bleeding end to end mightily.
Toward dawn I was summoned;
A jungle of tubes and bowls; going out big,
the symbols of mortician culture

blooming around like fungi.
He lay there weak as childhood.
They were filling him, an old sack,
with new wine. He took it darkly.
"When the wheat's ready for harvest,
draw it in," all I remember.
Strong enough behind his milky cat's eyes
to spin a trope about death, strong enough to live.
Foul January dawn
beetled down upon us, he lay there like a switchblade
awaiting the spring, awaiting death
like a palmed blade. No takers . . .

2.

Phil goes in chains to Harrisburg today
I sit here in the prison ward
nervously dickering with my ulcer
a half-tamed animal
raising hell in its living space.
Time to think once more of my father.
There were photos, brown, detailed
tintypes. You had only to look
(30, 40, years ago)
for the handsomest bucko present.
It was uncanny.
A head of burnished locks, a high brow
a cynic's sidelong look.
Boyo! You kept at center eye
the eye of storms.
In a mad Irish way "all there." Whole apple, one bite.
The mouth reminds me of a whip;
sensual and punishing.
Tasting the world, sexually alive,
calling the tune, paying the piper.
He was chaste as an Irish corpse,
Mother-maidensister-haunted.
We 6 were as much emblems of expiation
as of seasonal bedding

each of us sponsored by the church
like a first class relic or a nun's goody.

3.

I wonder tonight in Danbury Prison
in the damned off-season of human beings
an ulcer kicking at my groin
like the sour embryo of Nixon's next brainchild
I wonder—
the Jesuits staring 'round like frogs of the Nile
at baby Moses—
I wonder if I ever loved him
if he ever loved us
if he ever loved me;
an undersized myopic tacker
number 5 in pecking order
pious maybe, intelligent I guess
looking for corners where half in, half out
he could take soundings,
survive, emerge; protective coloration.
Not enamored of the facts of life
i.e., sledgehammers, chicken little,
the cracking muscles of the strong.
As a child you expect violence; the main issue
somehow to clear away
space and time
to survive in. Outside the circle, who cares?

He exacted performance, promptitude,
deference to his moods
the family escutcheon stained with no shit.
The game was skillful (we never saw it so well played
elsewhere), he was commonly considered
the epitome of a just man.
We sat on our perches blinking like six marmosets.
There were scenes worthy of Conrad,
the decks shuddering;
the world coming to end!

He is dead now.
The conduct of sons and priests
is not grist for news-hawks and kites.
When my mother (who surely
suffered most at his hands) read one account
served up by an esteemed scribe
she wept for shame and loss.
There is more honor, more
noblesse oblige, more
friendship with reality, more unconscious graceful wisdom
in the least gesture of her
little finger, than in
the droppings and screams of the whole preening profession
of whooping cranes.
The office of charity, of classic
Pietàs, fills the vacuum
around that absent figure
with the presence of compassion. My father—
when in '39 I braced and dug in
for the great leap, I was one
of 38 candidates for priesthood.
All excelled me
in arts, language, math,
self-assurance, the golden number of
the Jesuit dance. 32 years later
I sit in Danbury Prison for illegal
acts contrary to war.
Father
I close my eyes, conjure up
like a deaf-mute mimic
your ironic ghost. How convey
my gratitude, my sense
of the delicious rightness of things?
Whatever you denied us, you
gave us this, which enemies name
distemper, madness; our friends,
half in despair, arrogance.
Which I name, denying both—the best of
your juice and brawn, unified

tension to good purpose.
Prosit, requiescat.
The bad news drones on
plague after seventh plague
hypnotic, futile as an argument
for God's existence. . . .

5.

. . .
My father, asked what crop he grew
on the old farm outside Syracuse (depression
sour clay and drought); laconically:
boys! One year, an old mare dragging a harrow
through the sparse corn rows, with the perfect timing
of senescence
reached a drain ditch
near the roadside, stepped down daintily
as a duchess, lowered her backside,
lowered her long face to her knees (harness
jangling like rude jewelry) lay there
saying from her eyes; next move, yours.
Tonight under a paschal moon, I mimed
a Goya etching in the
prison yard
3 shadows coming, growing
came, grew, vanished like footpads—
Jesus, Satan, that interdicting
third, weaving, bargaining, up to his ears
in bloody Friday; Lord, is it I?
Under the shrewd exhalation of the moon,
I bundle up to throat; no
horse thieves, poachers,
informers in our blood! Nicked by his razor Dado
mutters in the mirror; *the blood of Irish kings*!
Mother at the stove, turns up her eyes to heaven . . .

7.

Dado's classical bent
left none unstigmatized. A white billy-goat

was marvelously misnamed, to fanfare
from the dog, faint horselaugh from the mare;
Ursus. He knocked the postman for a loop,
scattered mad Mamie Powell, chewed up,
in the side yard, until chased by sticks,
the shirt the '29 depression spared.
Crimes multiplying, stink
offending, he was sold off, reversing
the Judas trick, to metamorphose in paschal stew
in Little Italy, down country. We mourned him—
hooves, pride of blood, horns of
neighborhood dilemmas, nattering mouth, pirate's eye,
the uncouth unreconstructed thieving
alter ego of six boys.

1930; Dado decreed a mercy death.
A splay-legged spavined nag
bit the dust, under an orchard tree,
Tom firing point blank. Laziness
our virtue in common; we dug a shallow grave
heaped the cadaver over, like a
prairie cenotaph. One week later, mother,
stringing the laundry from tree to tree
was shaken to tears and flight. A colossal
long drawn fart issuing from the grave,
a strange unnatural
convulsion; earth heaved, ground opened,
a great equine rear leg shot up skyward.
The resurrection of the dead?
Weeks passed, sweet seasonal process
grounded the upstart sign, grounded my father's
Jovian lightnings . . .

8.

In the old fables
jays macaws jackals
cowardly inching forward careening hobbling jeering
surrounded the mysterious firebird.

The figure and form of the age.
Philip; the little blond boy with lowered eyes
in a blue fluted sweater
stands to the left of me in a faded kodak film, 1927.
You threw stones like a demon
hid your windup locomotive in the old grey immigrant trunk.
In one year your limbs telescoped out
a poet's brow, those commanding utterly blue eyes
a sapphire intensity, precision instruments taking
the world's size.

I do not know when the wager was first struck
I see another photo, a windy June day
outside Washington Shrine, the family smiling,
a single-minded triumph; its ordained priest!
war years, depression years decently buried in albums
then that "stampede into religion"
(John's sneering phrase)
the church's chased cup
continuity, rounded latinate
breaking up breaking up

Dado,
your sons
close kept in Danbury Jail
keep Maundy Thursday.
You lie close too
after the 90 year uphill climb.
Pompey graveyard, a "sylvan close"
(your phrase) of trees and mounds
slopes westward, gentle, sunny.
Are you proud of your 2 priests
plucked by the sovereign state, for crimes
against war crimes? The children of My Lai
like Fra Angelico's angels, make sport of death;
with instruments of harmony
keep green, for us, your grave.
Children—those natural buds
those nodes of process, rose red, snow white

first fruits of blood and semen, fallen rosy and white
to the spread aprons of women, fruits
of energetic love. Who strikes them—. . .

10.

Winters we chugged two miles to Sunday Mass
in a model-T snowbucker, old the year
it was born. Like a sailing fish it sported
flapping gills of isinglass and canvas.
We bedded down like Peter Rabbit's litter, crowded
in the hold, eyes, cold noses, Dado
pumping and worrying us along. Spread over all
6 boys, a 7 foot square Buffalo robe
gamey, coarse as porcupine. Arrived, dismounted
at St. John Baptist
we made an obedient huddle, awaiting
disposition of the steed. The robe, pulled from the rear seat,
made a splendid radiator noseguard
against deep freeze.

We sat at the children's Mass
singing from 5¢ notebooks the hymns
we murdered all week to Sister's beating stick
Mother dearest Mother fairest; to Jesus' heart all burning.
Monsignor McEvoy, our ample prophet, out of his
workday overalls (teacher, lawyer, builder)
splendid as an iconostasis, humble as Nazareth
gave us a children's gospel. Not bad; religion
stuck to our Sunday bones . . .
If we went mad, it was
for sweet reason's sake;
to wish all children well; to make of the world's breakup
cup, loaf, murder, horror, a first (or last) communion.
Once a year
New Year's Day, Mom and "the gang"
(Maggie's put-down) were summoned
to state dinner. I remember
straight chairs, straight talk, kids

frozen to our seats by the old maids'
steely looks; indifferent food, Maggie
dispensing into shirt pockets, on the hour
with a teaspoon, her stony pacifier, "Loft's Hard Candies."
They were straight out of Port Royal, Maynooth,
Oneida, pure as angels, proud as devils.
My father's marriage stuck in the throat of virtue.
Upchuck or swallow; the discreet dilemma
was audible for years, burp, cover up.

Grandmother Berrigan's portrait
looked down in mild wonderment,
a queen above a nest of bickering kites
she, troubled, questioning
the trick and treat of time's outcome—11 children, a widow on
Christmas day
of '74. Grandfather, bleeding
from immigrant's lung,
A daughter ran outside
to break the ice on the rain barrel, plunge a chunk
into his mouth. His body hauled
up scoured December hills in a democrat wagon
to lie where my father would lie.
Dado slept that day, a child
in a farm woman neighbor's arms . . .
I set this down
in Danbury Jail; Philip and I
priests, first (for all we know) to break
trust of the clan, trust
again and again, like Jansenius'
first rule of order; first pass-fail;
no one, not one of the
family, ever in jail.

11.

In old Assumption church on Salina Street
a phony dungeon on the dark rear stair
kept con Jesus under lock.

We crept down
during the long noon hour,
Lucifugae, sprats, beguiled
by darkness and vigil lights, prayed there
some better outcome for the man, caught in the twin
pincers of church and state. Would Pilate
dash the bowl to ground, would Caiaphas convert? . . .

Holy Saturday I set this down
by courtesy of the twin powers, doing time.
Jesus, lift head tonight from the foul grime
of churches. Thorns like bees
drone at the skull; does sacrifice bring in
straight on a beeline, honey, money, honor?
The dull eyes focus under a full moon
outside my window, resplendent
to frame a face in the informer's kiss. Who knows? Who knows?

a bargain struck
in silver, brings it down; rain, ruin
piece by piece, indictments on the 6
Harrisburg peacemakers, Berrigan et al
versus United States . . .
My grandmother's head
turns side to side, dubious as a ghost.
We teased mother.
Tom, Tom, the farmer's son,
why did you ever marry that one?—
(she blushed)
Indeed? He was considered quite a catch!

12.

November dawn, 1969, your jaw dropped, a semaphore
      the last train out of ghost town.
We gathered in 2 brown sacks
      everything you owned, an immigrant pauper's bundle

I leaned over the bed, breathing for you
      all that night long

(somebody else was there)
2 shadows over a fish tank
helpless as men watching the death
of the fish from whom
all men, fathers and sons, ad infinitum, come

A fish metamorphosing
into a father before our eyes—
hands, feet, blue as a fish

I could not take you in my arms, give you back
wits, volatile energy
confounding moods, appetite
the farm, drought, depression years
the scythe that whistled
like a wood plane across hard earth

Did you want it all back anyway?
Think. 6 sons, 5, 4, 3, 2, 1,—
then nothing, a wedding night, a bride
life awaiting doing all again?

You hated like hell that necessity
we lived by—your scant love
the stigma
it took years to heal; making do,
fear, damnation, fury.

Well we made it; some deep root of sanity
we sucked on. Above,
the idiot thrashing storms you made

Maybe it was your face dropping its mask
asleep over a book,
Irish intelligence; now and again
a piercing stab of virtue; a boy
kneeling beside you at Mass; a 6 yr. old
rocking-horse Catholic.

Thank you old bones, old pirate
 old mocker and weeper.
Could have lived to a hundred. But contrary passion
set in hard; falling downstairs
that last time, into your own
unconscious. To hell with it; bag it all.
a bloody act of the will, a fever nursed by rage. Sons
no longer mitigating presences, who
now and again had been;
 has been now. You turned to the wall.

And I have no recourse except
hatred and love, your hand
breaking through earth
nightmare or miracle;
your face
muffled in its shroud
a falcon
disdaining
the dishonor nailing
us here like stinking fish
(ancestors, sons)
to the world's botched cross

Landed, boned, buried in Pompey yard . . .
To see the performance, was scarcely
to believe it. One summer night
he tipped
the kitchen table, set for supper, up on end
for some supposed infraction. He fought sons
to a sullen draw, told enchanting children's stories
of summer nights, wrote poetry
like a flaring Turk, absurd, byronic,
battled the land to a dust storm,
prayed, slept stertorously in the big
leather rocker, ate like a demon,
exacted instant "yes sir! no sir!"
died like a sword swallower choked on
his breath's long blade . . .

The old house breathed relief
in his absence. None of us could, those years,
were screws turned on our thumbs, confess
to love him.
Was it that dearth of love
turned us to the long tragic way
on and on? What measure
of that irascible spirit, lodged unappeased
in us, bears, endures, survives—even Danbury? One virtue awaits
the arresting fist of death.
Until: Walk on, Take breath, Make do.

In blinding Minnesota winter sun
one of the older brothers
would hoist a kid up, pick-a-back, and run.
I was 3 or 4; John trundled me round the yard
ducked suddenly into a dark wood shed
striking me blind. Against my face
some rough pelted thing swayed frozen.
Recovering sight
screamed, screamed like a banshee, a child
gone mad for terror;
a frozen timber wolf's death-head
hung by a thong from the rafters, eyes open
bloody mouth—

The stuff of nightmares or of dental chairs.
In Danbury Clinic
I urge the wary inmates; *open wide now*; a superannuated
paraclete, all in white
for the liturgy; needles and drills
needles and drills. Domestic policy, we juice
America's pain to sleep

In the wink of an eye, graves shall open
the dead arise. Easter morning
I write: dearest mother, many friends
bring flowers to your bedside, smiles
from Danbury. We are well, our thoughts

are thanks. Thanks to you, the instrument
of truth, who plucked us by the hair
harebrain and all, from false peace. Alleluia.

NO ONE KNOWS WHETHER DEATH, WHICH MEN IN THEIR FEAR CALL THE GREATEST EVIL, MAY NOT BE THE GREATEST GOOD

It may be expedient to lose everything.
The moon says it, waxing in silence, the fruit of the heavens,
grape vine, melon vine.
Autumn upon us, the exemplar, the time of falling.
One who has lost all is ready to be born into all:
buddha moon socratic moon jesus moon
light and planet and fruit of all:
"unless the grain falling to earth die, itself remains alone"

A BIT OF HISTORY

Those Jesuit fathers (wrote Isaac Jogues from New France)
who purpose volunteering for these wilds
and the service of their Indian brothers
had best leave behind all regret for
university degrees, honors, prerequisites.
The questions raised by their clients will be other
than the subtleties their minds
sharpened and shone on, elsewhere.
TO WIT: can they bear heartbreaking portages
survive on sour pemican
live under intense extremes of heat, cold, solitude?
The times mitigate the questions, never quite stilling them.
As I learn, my middle cast cranium
bending to the intricacies, simplicities
of a new a b c.

SKUNK

The only fauna admitted
to the widespread country zoo
(every animal in his natural
habitat, no visible bars)
was an unloquacious
bumbling skunk.
He crept in under the full moon
like a moon thing, eyes
dazed, moonstruck. Limped
along unhandily, as though
on 5 feet or 3, footsore.
Looking for what?
We wished
he would breathe deep
as an ancestor, metamorphose
10 times his size
piss high as a Versailles fountain
his remarkable musk perfume.
We didn't want additional
prisoners, even dumb ones.
If they must come, atavistic,
mystical, then let them be
spectaculars, trouble-
shooters.   O skunk, raise
against lawnorder, your grandiose
geysering stinking *NO!*

WE WERE POOR POOR POOR

In prison remember
Dame Poverty, her strait uses;
Merton's photo, friend, confidant, brother under the skin
peering like young Picasso from the wall, a papery resurrection;
postcards, remnants
hung like the hanged from the cage wall.

Poverty: half your wits about you; the better half, a wife
gone off, a better offer.
O how fervently
we good burghers built jails, paid taxes for their upkeep.
Now they try us for size!
Brought down to size.   Procrustes broke us like cordwood.
"my tears   my tears   flow in the night"

REHABILITATIVE REPORT: WE CAN STILL LAUGH

In prison you put on your clothes
and take them off again.
You jam your food down
and shit it out again
You round the compound right
to left and right again.
The year grows irretrievably old
so does your hair burn white.
The mood; one volt above
one volt below survival,
roughly per specimen, space
sufficient for decent burial.

A DAY'S WORK IN THE CLINIC

I stand at the dentist's chair
hosing down
the havoc of his pincers
slow   slow
then a wider arc
he draws
the newborn tooth into light of day
Another day
another bloody day
root   limb   blind as bone
stillborn as a tooth

MEMORIES MEMORIES

In my ignorant salad days
(the middle 60's), the wife of the Sec. of Defense
earnest, elegant as a pompeian matron
supped next to me.   Much admired
for D.C. school reform   a committeewoman
of fervor
        her husband less admired
a cost product expert   hair slick as a beaver's
cold eyes instantly contracting to
the fleering public glare
            expanding
in the subterranean
warrens where he like a children's
animal tail
        disappeared around
this or that pentagonal corner

leaving the subaltern mice & moles
a-quiver to their nose hairs with
puritan anangke   O how
(wail) quite measure up?

Fridays the pentagon prayer room was crowded

In the postprandial mellow summer dark (quote)
"Mississippi is Vietnam.   When a people
reneges on joining the civilized world
you send in troops."
            Providence has assigned
sons and daughter to the estimable pair. My poem concerns
the death of children.

A VISITOR AWAITS THE PRISONER

You've got to hear that mechanical
ass or angel trumpeting; B E R R I G A N   2 3 7 4 2   Y O U
                                    GOTTA VISIT!

It rends the cell houses
in open summer, a mad circus dog
breaking the fiery barrier.
That voice's got no choices.
As if one whispered
shamefaced in paraplegic ears—
look mom, no hands,
feet, eyes, (balls even).

For the accession of the iron mongrel
to the rickety throne, the voice must be unconnected.
No brain box, attentive (say)
to the eloquent ignorance
of some young Socrates, hell-bent on manhood
savior potentially of the god-and-man damned
state. Better therefore, equivalently
dead, i.e., under lockup.

In place of manhood's precious filament and fuel bag—
Keys, their death rattle in the yard. How many points
of possession under law?
The hack, a nation state
bestrides the world.
Hear
that rehabilitating catechetic, one time more;
bellows the dog god; *priest, punk now*
who made the world?

13. Uncommon Prayer

WHO ARE WE, THAT YOU TAKE NOTE OF US? / *PSALM 8*

Through all the universe
your glorious name resounds

I raise eyes
to the lofty tent of the heavens
sun   stars   moon
foil of your right hand

I see rejoicing
beast and dolphin
eagle, cormorant, condor
triumphant plowing the seas
in the plangent air godlike

I bend to the faces of children
they lisp your name

And I ponder;
mere mortals, who are we
that you
take note of us
have care of us?

fragile, fallible
vermicular, puny—
crowned now, sceptred now
conscious now, exultant now!

Through all the universe
how glorious is your name!

THEY CALL YOU BLIND MAN: CALL THEIR BLUFF / *PSALM 10*

Lord, why   stand on the sidelines
silent as the mouth of the dead, the maw of the grave—
O living One, why?

Evil walks roughshod, the envious set snares
high and mighty the violent ride
Applause for maleficence, rewards for crime
Yourself set to naught

Eyes like a poniard impale the innocent
Death cheap, life cheaper
The mad beast is loosened, his crooked heart mutters
Fear only me!

Lord, they call you blind man. Call their bluff

extinguish their envy

See; the poor are cornered
marked for destruction, grist
for a mill of dust

At the bar of injustice
they tremble, wind-driven birds
under the beaks and stares
of the shrouded Big Ones—
No recourse but you; no recourse
but your faithful love!

ALL DAY I CRY OUT TO YOU / *PSALM 22*

Eloi Eloi lama sabacthani
My God my God, why have you turned from me?
all day I cry out to you
all night no end to my plaint

But you are silent, are absent
you, the hope of our fathers
the tenderest of mothers
They called out and you answered them
never in vain their half uttered prayer

As for me, I crawl the earth like a worm
a zero, of no account, none.
The great ones look askance
their glances pierce me through
a man made of air

They nudge one another,
palaver behind their hands: there goes the fool
He took his oath to a blank page, he cast his bread
to the dogs, he trampled the law of the land
Now shall God bail him out?

My midwife you were, you drew me
out of the guts of my mother
Red as a budded rose I lay
at your breast and hers
You held me at knee, your first born

My life is pure nightmare
my days are a dance of death
nights a welter of beasts
they circle me, hem me in
(self-concocted, self-sprung
from forehead and groin, my fears
my self-will expended, compounded)
Do I live? I lunge toward death
die? I am cast in the arms of sheol.

My veins run in full flood
my bones are a random fall
my heart melts like a snow
my tongue is a rattling gourd
hands and feet a criminal prey—

crucified to a tree I stand, naked
to mockers. They perch there unblinking
birds of prey
They number my bones
a skeleton sprinkled with lime

O save me my savior! as once you drew me
from the womb of oblivion

bring to a second birth
out of hell's gut, this hapless one.

INTO HIS RIGHT HAND / *PSALM 33*

SECURITY SECURITY, the plain chant of the damned.
Border guards, guard dogs, gun sights
an investiture of death. Yet

what its so vulnerable as we,
who cave in at a blow
who fall like kicked sacks?

we die in an hour, insects, flowers
we drift down wind, we are shadows in armor
death our portion, our menu, our bleak house;

And the God of life? he took clay
like a master potter, heart shaped clay
fired it with his breath. And we stood there

children, people, animals, insects and flowers.
The diurnal planets
he set spinning on his fingertips, let them go
Like a feather, down wind.

See, brutes huff and puff
they rake the world with fire
they build hecatombs
of shuddering bones

The Lord of life
keeps them at edge of eye
half attentive
no need of his

vengeance, judgment;
they crumble like a
faulty tower
down wind
at center eye
the apple of his eye
blossoms, swells, ripens
—the faithful who fall
straight as a plumb line
into
his right hand.

OUR KARMA IS NEAR / *PSALM 58*

The brahmins enter
dressed to kill
ermine and periwigs

sober as mourners
mouths like the grave
"justice their errand"

Crooked in spirit
skilled in deceit
merciless of tongue

they stop their ears
lest they be chastened, shed
of their venomous ways

Then fall on them, vengeance!
break their bones
open their veins
Off the earth's face with them
aborted, inhuman
grant them no light of day!

Tempests carry them off
root, branch and thorn!

The joy of the just is this;
an end of injustice.
He exults, he washes his limbs
in the blood of the wicked

Shout it; our karma is near!
mockers, God is not mocked!

SHOW ME YOUR FACE, O GOD / *PSALM 61*

At land's end, end of tether
    where the sea turns in sleep
        ponderous, menacing
            and my spirit fails and runs
        landward, seaward, askelter

            I pray you
                make new
            this hireling heart
                O
                turn your face to me
            —winged, majestic, angelic—

                    tireless,
                        a tide
                my prayer goes up—
            show me your face, O God!

A MERCY, A HEALING / *PSALM 64*

I walk in your world
a mercy, a healing—

Like a cooper of barrels
you bind the mountains with ribbing

your hand rests on rambunctious seas
they grow peaceful
the brow of a sleeping child

Autumn is a king's progress
largesse lies ripe on the land

up, down the furrow your midas touch
rains gold;
rainbows arc from your glance

Fall of rain, evenfall, all all is blessing!

STILL I WOULD BE YOUR FAITHFUL SERVANT / *PSALM 88*

I hear
only
the closing of doors
the turning of locks.
Friends
(friends?)
freeze at sight of me.
Is this your doing?
misfortune my middle name?

They pass by, heads airborne
supernal on worldly business—
priests, pariahs, making it big
passing the buck, concocting
pie in the sky.

Day and night I cry out to you
No other, no help for me.
Come then, samaritan—

Out of sight, out of mind
I wander this no man's land

The living
wash hands of me
the dead
close eyes against me
Worse;
You
turn away.

The thought of death crosses me—
cold comfort.
What comfort to you
my death
that cold shoulder
that icy touch—

In hell who praises you?
who magnifies your deeds?
          hell's chorus
spontaneous, breathless
striking up
Alleluia Alleluia?

Still I would be
[misfortunate, maladroit]
your faithful servant

Yet
day after day
your blows rain down

You winnow my friends
they vanish like chaff
you leave me
for only
familiar—

night

RESCUER, CONSOLER, FRIEND / *PSALM 94*

Happy the one you raise up Lord
to esteem your law
evil days will not touch him

But the wicked—
their thoughts are a mockery, this God
sees nothing, hears nothing, says nothing!

They carry heads high
They weave cunning words. To hear them talk
oppression, war mongering
greed, duplicity, were noble endeavors!

In kangaroo courts, the just
they condemn out of hand

Law And Order! they cry
lawlessness, disorder, all their skill.

God of strict requital, judge them!
Lest they prevail forever
mockers, mimics of justice
torturers, liars
piling their booty sky-high
on the bowed backs of the poor . . .

There is one who speaks for me
There is one who judges in justice
When an evil snare all but trips me
He, rescuer, consoler, friend

will utterly destroy them

To me, he has shown another face—
rescuer, consoler, friend.

I LOVE YOUR PROMISE / *PSALM 119*

A double heart be far from me, Lord
I love your commands
my hope is your promise

A lying tongue be far from me
I love your promise
my hope is your law

Far from me a violent will
your will is my hope
I love your commands

To witness your law
to love your commands
be my first love.

MAY I TO MY LORD HASTEN / *PSALM 131*

Lord cut my cloth
to a human measure—
big schemes, big follies
the dark ground of connivance
be far from me

Come my soul
like a bird to the hand
like a child to breast
I will nurture you, mother you

As my soul hastens
to breast, to hand
may I to my Lord
hasten. Abide.

HAND IN HAND, HEART IN HEART / *PSALM 133*

Sisters and brothers dwell in peace
What joy, what an omen!
Hand in hand, heart in heart
a double strength

A waterfall pausing, various, ever moving,
roses, surprising strawberries
A closed circle, an enclosed garden, a universe—

There
war's hoarse throat is silenced
and praise goes up night and day
and the stanchions of slaves in the hills
gather dust, spring ivy.

14. The Discipline of the Mountain

THE BEGINNING

It was that day the Christian heart
(stalled between hope and hell)
missed beat—
that day Christ confounded
death and hell
His siege perilous
hardly begun was over

This day this day
my journey began out of this world
(deeper into this world)
I would penetrate
the lying semblances the feverish fits and starts
the chimeras stalking appetites
(the ghastly smiles switch blades of my street)
that dark muddled sack
the modern world

a journey
a task
—to learn from the dead—
A mountain exigent dangerous
honeycombed like a Hopi village
with weird eyeless all seeing tribes
building like starfish new limbs organs souls
dormant ignored unused on earth
feverishly misused on earth

Having come to a middle ground
a measure of dry wisdom
totted up resources
Had come through
the whiff of hell the taste of death
detention courts public spectacle
Time to move on. Time
moved on. Time said
Move On.

Dante pilgrim of that mountain
mover of imagination
eloquent unitive
He leaps from the page like a
winged foot on the uphill climb

Him I choose for guide mentor; *Come with me*
brother near saint near hero
Irony disclaimer
lend savor to the soul
I pray; Do not take me

too seriously
In thin air do not confuse
real world with errant
appetitive psyche Confusion in such matters
works great mischief
I summoned him intoning
Per correr migliori acque alza le vele
omai la navicella del mio ingegno,
lascia dietro a sé mar sì crudele

He stood before me modern spirit
soul of wit and fire benign quicksilver
but stern too a face the dead put on
soul's final form

That beginning!
in a meadow
where the mountain started upward
like a turbulent thought
clouding the brow of God
In that meditative meadow
on a spring morning
the Almighty
took counsel with himself—
then
an encompassing gesture—

So be it! death no dominion!
I will raise him up!

In that meadow
my Dante light and truth
spread his hands
in pure dew
anointed me
sealing signing my condition—
pilgrim of the absolute

We climbed laboriously that rock face
sun at our backs sun ahead a weird sun dance
between huff and puff I spoke to my friend
Will the journey always be arduous?
Only at first Time will come
when the sheer levels off Finally thc passage so eases
you'd think yourself drifting summering downstream.
Still we dragged ourselves upward upward
a ledge stood under our feet
There we sank speechless exhausted

THE ENTRANCE

We came to a portal
Stern unbending an angel acosted
What errand brings the living
out of due time among the dead?
His short sword clove the air
stopped us in our tracks
I knelt seven times his blade traced
a serpentine S on my forehead
Blood tears fell on my face
Welcome to dolor
to glory

We entered The gates clapped to
like the two hands of God
ordaining ends and beginnings.

IMAGES OF THE CARVEN WALL

The height of that mountain!
A cleft in the rock—
like blind moles or the newborn
We rode a surf of stone   it bore us
this way and that its own sharp will
The moon was down
we stepped out   sheer face of stone
and the void

That promontory wall
        carved so cunningly
it seemed the mute stone spoke

First an angel   bent to a matchless maid
you would have sworn   *hail Mary*
breathed from his lips   She in turn
spoke   or nearly so   *behold the Lord's servant*

Further   a tumultuous scene
a cart   a span of white oxen
the sacred ark   the holy city
King David   lowly afoot
whirled   danced like a Sufi

THE PROUD BROUGHT LOW

As in a sweating distressful dream I saw them
        poor burdened souls plodding along
                enslaved;
pride of place   pride of birth   pride of achievement

            There on the first terrace
                they expunged the first sin
                    purged away
    the furious inflated emptiness of the world

Aloft in stone
grotesque grimacing figures
knees against chin bore the brunt
of roof tree or ceiling—
these rocks were real these souls
bent double bore their incongruous
useless burdens
round round
the solitary track

Their only prayer—

Our Father free to love and be loved
praised be your name even in this place
The peace of your kingdom come
(helpless we to bring its coming)
Angelic wills bow before you
so may our own
In the dread wilderness of this world
deprived of you
every step
is a fool's wayward ring-around
We forgive all wrongs Do you
also forgive us
Our strength turns to water
pour us not out a waste

A FRIEND BROUGHT LOW

One groaned aloud as though the rock he bore rubbed him raw
he shifted the huge weight like an ox
In that place of bondage
peered at me knew me called to me
Brother mine the chaos of the world is stilled here
time like a puff of wayward wind
eon upon eon
less than a blink of God's eye
Our egos once blared in public places

that flourish is stilled
death stops all throats
In this gyre we turn beasts of burden
beating to dust the flowers beneath our feet
that once like fame and name were green and gold by turn

I said shamefaced
The truth you grasp and give
pricks my great pride as well
But say for my instruction
how were you saved
if pride rode you to the end
to bleed and race and win
the dead leaves of the laurel?

He answered
In my city my name
stood big as a billboard
superfluous honors
rained down a paper storm
But I saw in nightmare
the Kingdom of mad dogs
the Bomb raining down
black rain world's end

My family myself
decked out beribboned
like demon dolls
indentured to hell

To the town square I went
stood like a madman
in rags and ash
miming begging pardon
for obeying to the jot
the law of the damned
for neglect of that good
named God

Rejoice with me!
from slavery I came
from hell   from self will
into my freedom

THE ANGEL OF HUMILITY

An angel approached
arms open in greeting then
he touched   barely touched
my forehead   *The way   be easier now.*
Indeed the way eased
or was it rather
lightening
of soul's gross baggage?

Like one who all unheeding
bears on his person   some mark or brand
and reads   only in others'
amusement or dread
how awry he walks—
I put hand to my forehead—
That welt and wound
assuaged   part healed!

A choir of souls
struck up my soul's
breakthrough—
Blessed the poor in spirit!

CHRIST AND THE CHURCH

About that center   a scene unfolded
like a living rose—
adorers   believers
former hucksters   highwaymen and whores
Priests who bore the single mind

the fervent eye of discipleship
and clerics like pears and pigs once rutting and rotting
and parents devout children milling like colts
and captains of the world uneasy and creaking in their
straitjackets (loosed now that suffocating power)
and factions and fictions first world second world third
world
they marched into the circle their banners
many tongued
Si Vis Pacem, Prepara Bellum!
The slogans crossed out; the banners read simply: *Dona
Nobis Pacem.*
Then in silk suits, discreet brief cases, bankers and
dealers their abstracted look like engraved faces on dollars
and artists mountebanks musicians jugglers mimes
word charmers gurus false and true
then multitudes of nobodies like schools of fish shaped
like one great shimmering ichthys like multitudes of
migrating birds
in shape of one great sky darkening bird
gentle all but faceless folk their eyes spoke for
them their
artless adoration "Lord how good to be here"
Then a pride of popes Popes good and
indifferent a weary millennial look bowed
under the weight of mystery apprehended mystery
betrayed
And here and there like lamplighters in a dead city souls
to whom
one could entrust his soul intent on the One
who above all others was found faithful
Then tycoons red of face congested of throat like sacks of
money
tied and tagged
They came hand in hand with the poor who spoke for them
sponsored them—
Is this enough?
That vast pushy dusty hungry unchurched
fervent throng

hoping against hope believing and faithless (once) selling out and
buying in (formerly) chin up and hang dog
And after all (the time is close to after all) this in their favor—
they are not formless drifters spinning with shift of tide
or wind
but a vast yeasty ferment
an epicenter true point and eye simplicity itself
The weird overhead process of fish and bull virgin and scales
neither defines nor deflects their
Purpose!
hints invitations inklings
They shift from foot to foot bear heat and thirst
a mix and muddle of creation recognizable to anyone
who is part of it longs to be part of it
And then
always those few comparatively few
who must not be lost sight of though they have neither skill
nor will at commanding attention
for our sake and theirs must not be lost sight of—
The prisoners for justice' sake the martyrs the naysayers
the intractable ones
the irreformable unrehabilitatable ones
those who under every sun political flags the spasm of crowds
of jutjawed bemedaled mobsters
keep a kind of Last Day Cool
an unswipeable smile
a passionate distance
from Blah and Blight and The Next Hard Riding Messiah
Over the Hill
Let us accord honor let us make way for these they file
toward the center

In rags and stripes and newly struck chains
No tigers griffins heroes
Nonetheless the throng makes way for them
dividing itself in two a divided sea

See!   after endless years
sons   sisters   friends
from exile delivered   from gulags   from kangaroo
courts   from torture   from
    unjust sentence   from seizure of fortune
from Devil's Islands   from Siberias   from tiger cages
    from interrogation centers   from ghettoes   reserves
from colonels and shahs and juntas and sheriffs delivered
from starvation delivered
and above all   beyond all   miracle of all
from death delivered!
See now
in the grey faces
and skinny bones
and silence long as the spool of the fates—
here   the human venture vindicated!
Here   the philosopher's stone and
Lost Atlantis and
Shangri-la and
modest utopia!

They near
The Lord looks up   the multitude folds in   like
    living dough
How long O Lord   how long?   has been their plaint
Now   This moment   His look   somber
    self collected   the look of one who   endures
    comes through (but barely)—
that look breaks the glacial will of God
They embrace   one after another
Tears   laughter   two weathers
    contending in one sky

15. May All Creatures Live

CONSOLATION

Listen
if now and then
you hear the dead
muttering like ashes
creaking like empty
rockers on porches

filling you in   filling you in

like winds in empty
branches   like stars
in wintry trees
so far
so good

you've mastered finally
one foreign tongue

OFFERING

What I offer is
spontaneous
life, soap,
operas, death
& above all & so to speak
mystical effluence

Often mistaken
for God almighty
I am blessed with
the 6th sense of his archangel
with portfolio,
namely humor—
a trap falling
like capital death NOW!
an explorer's prow
knifing the beach HERE!

I hereby name
the river that flows
inevitably, and after
meanderings, maybes

                    —in confluence
Consequence.

TO CHRIST OUR LORD

To believe
you have to disbelieve
unstitching like love's sweet
cheat, the day's meticulous rainbow

But these, jackals
on the spoor of jackals
eat you like dead bees
for lust of the honeycomb
scatter you, death's parade.

Then priests wheel in like bears on unicycles
overtrained, underpaid—
like motorized brooms they love debris
their vocation;
          bees' husks, taffeta remnants
confetti, all that's left
of the dead parade

O golden goose named Pharoah
          they made you glorious
               only for their kitchen—
   for lust of the savory
      paté ROMANITA

               Roman goose
      guardian of San Angelo
            honking the devils off the sacred
                              precincts

we found you dead & scattered
for lust of a golden egg
no sooner born
than closed, clouded like an eye
You brood there in the dark
like your own egg
you glimmer there in the dark like a
world ransoming pearl—

like a petrified tree
your heart of stone
your gospel a stone
you
an argument against God's existence
and the jackals chorus—
if he were not if he were not

Unto myself then! I step back back back
what is done is undone
what is believed is disbelieved

I whisper
like the first day of winter
disbelieve!
and close my eyes
like a wintry animal
and stop my heart in its shroud
and forbid life, and life giving metaphors.

SUPPOSITIONS

The frailest of suppositions
keep me afloat—
Imagine a man walking the watery path
the dolphin's cunning opens,
straight toward me.

Frail suppositions
keep me testing the air—

Imagine a voice
undeflected, at hand—
Follow Me!

A frail supposition
keeps me sane on the earth
Imagine someone walking ahead
beckoning me on—

For such a one I take my next clown tumble!

COLD COMFORT MUMBO JUMBO

Like medicos in league with morticians
staving death off purportedly but

beckoning him in behind you

They smile, their tests
show all clear, you're home free

Meantime they're phoning
the priest, the police, the panic squad

the insurance agent, the obit
page of the NY Times

Meantime? my time.
Laughing like gas I straighten my tie

hug myself in the glass

love you kid, stout heart, sound lungs
first class unborn death

AMBITION

I wanted to be useless
as life itself; so

I told the president so
and told the pope so
and told the police so

& one & all chorused
like furies, like my friends
And who told you so?

The dead told me so
the near dead; prisoners
all who press faces
against a pall of ice
against a wall of glass
a grave, a womb's thrall.

I read their lips, alas.
I told the poem. So.

O CATHOLIC CHURCH

I could love you more if
you mothered me less, if you
egged on like a shrew by expensive shrinks
and your own shrinking shadow
weren't such an
Amazon of Order

Let me tell you my dream; a
circus act. I'm performing
under the tent's navel, swinging out
over and over, hundreds of feet up;
one half million eyes down there

can't believe the act. And you're the
anchor rope, the
lynch pin, the
center pole

No; better, it's
your act and mine!
skills, courage perfectly mutual—
tonight you're on my shoulders;
the long horizontal pole vibrates with the subdued
energy, passion, anguish of the world;
north pole to south
horrendous, exultant news passing through
your hand and mine—
and we move
and we move it
and we are moved

One body, vertical, functional, ecstatic—
a figure of the future?
a window of Chartres Cathedral
evangelists on the shoulders of prophets.

Then sometimes I dream you're the north star.

And (this is no dream)
though I am forced to eat papier maché for breakfast
and fret for the death of my friends
served up like cat and dog food
to alley cats, to mad dogs—
noble souls whose only offense is
they resist the recycling of kangaroos into
the elegant eclair shit of
Park Avenue pimps

Still dear friend, if
you are the north star
please say so now and then;
not incessantly
not with a xerox blizzard from outer space
no, only a word
from a starry mouth
heard softly here and there
with authority too

—a forefinger pointing
—a voice saying 'north'

We could infer the other directions;
south, east, west; and their
finer divisions, down to the hairlines

But bickering, meandering, not knowing
Do not from doughnut, north from south—
this is our madness!

And you could relieve it!
Pope John, from northern Italy, once helped.

APRIL SHOWERS MAY COME YOUR WAY

I walked or stood appalled in my city
(the slovenly poor
fouling their nest
the broad beamed academics
sterile, decorous
women snarling, drunks, crazies
New York wilfully falling
down its own bung hole)

Suddenly
the city stirred, its
deep veins trembled
flowed free.
After winter savagery
sweet breathed April.

I saw the city new;
Epiphany; a small child
in a grassy place
entirely beautiful and alone

For an hour no one died. All, all were born.

TO MY MOTHER (I)

Don't Die

Everything memory heightens
I want green again

the cow and the cow's turd
the Phoenix N.Y. streetcars

zinging along like cater-
pillars on roller skates

your shopping bags   your finery
your vintage squirrel coat

grandma's garden   her greenhorn
Black Forest brogue

Green it!   Sweet, we'll chirrup
like God's green grasshoppers
on beds of 4 leaf clover

Only the dead get hauled
dry as John the Baptist's
kosher closing eye
off to die.

TO MY MOTHER (2)

Wonder

no wonder that you
whose spirit life long

dug in   touched stone

dying
yield up

a flower a spice
rare rare to the sense

TO MY MOTHER (3)

A New Child Named For You

Whether
archaic *Frida*
survived or not, of no moment
to a dying woman—
caprice of time
diminishing you
small smaller and shortly
a memory

Then lo!
the witless child
raised fingers of dawn
her tongue incanting
the enfeebled the diminished the dead
cried
Frida I am Frida

TO MY MOTHER (4)

Unlike

the blind know you
the halt the lame
the dead who pass

like air through us—

unlike unlike
ourselves who pass
mad as a blade

through air or you

and run you through

TO MY MOTHER (5)

Passage

One night or another
while daft souls sailed off
on broom sticks,
gathering moon moss,
scavenging
in dark closets

you rise from sleep
comb your waist long hair
quietly quietly
(children asleep in the house)

room to room, touch
the moonstruck faces of children

open the outer door
which of itself closes

step into
become
that light

TO MY MOTHER (6)

Honeymoon

Not much talk of it
Wrong planet wrong flavor
you'd say quirkily

Still
something unexpected a sign—

I remember one day
a transfiguring look

the secret indrawn sweetness
an old wife bestows
backward like an heirloom
(despite time, that murderous blunderer)
on a new bride

Recall it today
Block Island roses
fog the noonday
like a windfall
of butterflies—

I was a June bride
we huffed away from the wedding
on the Northern Minnesota Rail Road.
I sat there enthroned—
mile upon mile wild roses.

ACCOUNTS

Taking into account all kinds of things
from the state of the economy

to the state of the union
to the state of amnesia

to the state of my fate

which like 50 or more states
(kids can name them)
is like

a gang rape
in a swedish nursery
or a fire drill in hell—

Will someone please inform me
precisely when
I died

or why that
departure, arrival
is

by recorded announcement
put off
and off
and off

LIFE, SO TO SPEAK

Please walk me awake
foot dragging, shambling
a druggie in a mad dream of needles

I'll come out of it
I'll come out of it

but only
if you massage
a chicken heart
into love's heat and beat

Mother
I'll walk again
brother
I'll walk again

Yell it out
I'm deaf as a doughnut

Deal it out
keep flipping
deuces wild
to the blue hands
of the near dead

A VISIT TO THE BOOK OF KELLS AND A WALK IN THE PARK

A kick of wind
like the left hind leg
of the ghost of a dog—
lickety split
the brown leaves go

then
leaves lie quiet
the wind chases itself
elsewhere.

Under glass, in Met museum
this day I saw
a bird of paradise
outspread
the grandiose, grotesque
book of Kells.

Come wind, let us die easy
come book, let us live forever.

ZEN POEM

How I long for supernatural powers!
said the novice mornfully to the holy one.
I see a dead child
and I long to say, *Arise!*
I see a sick man
I long to say, *Be healed!*
I see a bent old woman
I long to say, *Walk straight!*
Alas, I feel like a dead stick in paradise.
Master, can you confer on me
supernatural powers?

The old man shook his head fretfully.
How long have I been with you
and you know nothing?
How long have you known me
and learned nothing?
Listen; I have walked the earth for 80 years
I have never raised a dead child
I have never healed a sick man
I have never straightened an old woman's spine

Children die
men grow sick
the aged fall
under a stigma of frost

And what is that to you or me
but the turn of the wheel
but the way of the world
but the gateway to paradise?

Supernatural powers!
Then you would play God
would spin the thread of life
and measure the thread
5 years, 50 years, 80 years
and cut the thread?

Supernatural powers!
I have wandered the earth for 80 years
I confess to you,
sprout without root
root without flower
I know nothing of supernatural powers
I have yet to perfect my natural powers!

to see and not be seduced
to hear and not be deafened
to taste and not be eaten
to touch and not be bought

But you—
would you walk on water
would you master the air
would you swallow fire?

Go talk with the dolphins
they will teach you glibly
how to grow gills

Go listen to eagles
they will hatch you, nest you
eaglet and airman

Go join the circus
those tricksters will train you
in deception for dimes—

Bird man, bag man, poor fish
spouting fire, moon crawling
at sea forever—
supernatural powers!

Do you seek miracles?
listen—go
draw water, hew wood
break stones—
how miraculous!

Listen; blessed is the one
who walks the earth 5 years, 50 years, 80 years
and deceives no one
and curses no one
and kills no one

On such a one
the angels whisper in wonder;
behold the irresistible power
of natural powers—
of height, of joy, of soul, of non belittling!

You dry stick—
in the crude soil of this world
spring, root, leaf, flower!

trace
around and around
and around—
an inch, a mile, the world's green extent,—
a liberated zone
of paradise!

VISION

(after Juliana of Norwich)

then showed me he
in right hand held
everything that is

the hand was a woman's
creation   all lusty
a meek bird's egg

nesting there   waiting
her word   and I heard it

newborn   I make you
nestling   I love you
homing   I keep you

COME NOW, CHOOSE

The eye regards the
   heart, a western view
   The heart regards
   the eye, the Chinese
   say

and the great world
between—
both
known by
caliper and transfus-
ion rigor and gift.
I suppose I must
in western fashion
choose
among methods
but I cannot

SPIRIT EXPLAINED TO A CHILD

breath   bird
shuttle   sword
weaving us
wanting us

the morse code
of the stalled
dead
what
dry stick doesn't
and tall cock does

st elmo's fire
in the bones of saints

blind man's bluff
called for once

the goose's blood
on the fox's grin

3 seraph wings
over my eyes
turn   turn   turn

EMULATION

The world's tallest sun flower
doesn't know it;
could equally be
a flea on the nit picked
rear of a wart hog.

Once it knows, a price lies
presto! on its magisterial head;
like that Sun King who prided himself
out of this world. *Snip snip*
scissors, snicker snee. The golden

flower of the day falls, all disarray.

SEPTEMBER 27, 1971

A chinese ideogram
shows someone
standing
by his word.
Fidelity. Freedom
consequent
on the accepted
necessity of
walking where
one's word
leads.
Wherever.
Hebrew prophets and
singers also
struck the theme;
bodies belong
where words
lead
though the com-
mon run of exper-

ience be
that stature
shrinks as
the word
inflates.
The synthesis;
no matter what (or
better) *never*
the less

COMPASSION

The sun comes, goes
driven from heaven by a wild fog

that drives the island too, a ghost ship
or a painter's stroke; here, away.

The island exists, the sun exists; illusion
or relation? both

in degree. Compassionate, the truth
illumines the common meadow

—only now, only a moment—

warms
in the stem of a weed
life and its life line; poetry.

A DYING GULL ON THE BEACH

He sat there, kingly and cognitive
wings lax
on the nest egg death
One eye followed me

a diamond on a pivot.
I thought; there's a brain need never cry;
Daniel
translate my dream !

Though my name
is known here and there
and I peddle the I Ching
as God peddles the book of Daniel

No thank you

(hotfoot gingerly by.)
I know
therefore I am;
well
just
barely

AGAIN, THE DYING GULL

How comfort you? O let me
bear you a renovated economy
dust free as a flag

wax sprayed like the presidential desk
big as a closet where the dead
hang their great coats; or

the pope's throne that is built up
of the bones of saints.

Let me bring you the cure for cancer, though
presumably like old Tithonus your
mortal trouble is other. Or
a cup of hemlock. Or no, a dollar bill

inflated like a rubber raft to
bear you to the Blessed Isles. O what do you require?

Apple pie? a dark psalm?
hell on wheels?
an amulet? a war on poverty?
ozone belt? vitamins?

I know a medic on West 98 Street noted for
transfusions; root, resin
blue blood, murky incantations.

We could hurry there; quick,
I will carry you in my green cap.

Please, there is time, do not fear
come to America and be healed.

YET AGAIN THE DYING GULL AND PRESIDENT FORD

Shame on you
dying easy   when our president
earnest as a rosecrucian, his poll
lit like a holy pumpkin

gives with his
stentorian barfing upbeat,
a pigskin hero whiffing
the steam and liniment of eternity

shame on you   you never had a wife
sliced up like mushrooms
and 200 million sullen pushcarts
piled with unborn apples like red eyes
waiting in the wings for the right wrong

YOU MIGHT CALL THIS A LOVE POEM

Everything Californian—
high extravaganza.
They prod you like a captive
Mohawk brave or bear—
Who's there
inside the pelt, or under
the savage hues and feathers?

I walk through California
eternally a misfit—
grey, gringo, amid fireworks
by Berlioz or Wagner.
Incurably blond, gigantic
landsmen take to the surf—
the skiffs head in like hounds
landward, on the spoor
of pure catastrophe.

SALVATION

Crossed the Susquehanna in twilight
Rowers, their oars majestic as Pharoah's, a
watery V for a wake. Calm, calm
like ghosts of geese moving north, honking the
end of the ice age upstream

Off to a poetry reading, I add these words to
my store
like a pinch penny Pharoah in the sixth of seven lean
years

For I think tonight of wheat
of the parched mouth
the long stony stare of the dead

Wave these words before my eyes, they will
unfixate

Wrap my heart in these, tote it home
it will melt in your mouth
Hold this mirror
If your face shows there
mine will dawn, recognition

Shout in my ear your name
I will hear that feathery long distance voice
will resurrect and run—
mistaking (but not really)
a scotch on the rocks
for salvation bells.

HARM NOT THE TREES
(Rev.,c.7,v.3)

Down, it comes down.
A sawdust column
dissolves
in choked air.

Roots splayed out level,
a huge starfish, a silver star
like the one inset in marble
in Bethlehem grotto; Hic Jesus Natus Est
who died on a tree.

This wooden star
sprung from convulvuses, wet
with a hundred rings of life
the tears of Jesus, a pathetic fallacy
for times tragic, awry.

three or four weeks of spring,
when in southland, mocking birds toss
sleepless with ecstasy.

O may all creatures live!

FIDELITY

Coming up Broadway, a fruitless evening
reception at U.N., the 'revolutionary ambassador'
resounding like a stale ash tray or like
the secretary of any state you mention & reflecting

sadly, the old game starts again
before the bloody flag is hoisted dry.
Life's an Orson Welles turn out of Graham Greene;

The train rushes on, our hero in fatigues
saunters down the careening aisle
of the third class carriage
expansive, macho
he disappears into mirrors

Minutes later he stands there—
diplomat's stripes, strictly first class
stiff as a sword cane. He's hardened, molten to mirror.

Alas folks, freaks, minority spirits, we've lost again.
It rains on Broadway, tears of knowledge.
I look for a store to buy a pen to blacken and blear
a page, tears or rain. I'll walk to 104th Street

where my old friend the picture framer
propped a photo of his dead wife in the window.

Rain worsens
Knowledge goes under

He was inefficient and faithful
she, propped in a wheel chair like a cauliflower
in a stall, months and months. Every hour or so

lit a cigarette
put it to her lips;

One day
a crazy old black woman
named by me, Crazy Horse
came by
leaned convivially over

the speechless mindless creature, yelled
'How are you dearie?' and kissed her like a luv.

I've long pondered fidelity. You can't know
even Gerald Ford that lethal dummy, might be snatched
from mad comics by his cancerous wife. When the old woman
grew hopelessly ill, he closed the cramped
musty curiosity shop at 2 PM each day, took a taxi

to Misericordia Hospital
sat there at bedside
all evening. One day
slight good news;
'She ate something, they've

stopped the intravenous feeding.' A merciful interlude only;
she died that night in his arms. On this foul foot path
mule track, death mile, oblivion alley, bloody pass
Broadway, pith and paradigm of the world, cutting the
50 States of Amnesia like a poisoned pie; a swollen Styx
an Augean drain ditch

a lotus blooms.

He looked up grey faced as I came in. 'She went peacefully
your green plant was a comfort.' Still, wishing I could
summon

for myself, for my friends, someday

for the world at large—
yes the self damned
the hypocrites, the power brokers
the 'revolutionary ambassadors'

a bare whiff of that bloom

hand laid on hand signifying a sacrament.

When I edged in sideways
past the morose dying
woman, her wheelchair
lodged like an embolism
in the body politic,
her skin
wrapped like a rodent's
in a moth eaten muff
I came not off magical Broadway
into Ripoff Boutique—
but where
springs have source

stream meeting stream signifying a sacrament.

PROPHECY

The way I see the world is strictly illegal
to wit, through my eyes

is illegal, yes;
to wit, I live
like a pickpocket, like the sun
like the hand that writes this, by my wits

This is not permitted
that I look on the world
and worse, insist that I see

what I see
—a conundrum, a fury, a burning bush

and with five fingers, where my eyes fail
trace—

with a blackened brush
on butcher sheets, black on white
(black for blood, white for death
where the light fails)

—that face which is not my own
(and my own)
that death which is not my own
(and my own)

This is strictly illegal
and will land me in trouble

as somewhere now, in a precinct
in a dock, the statutes
thrash in fury, hear them
hear ye!
the majestic jaws

of crocodiles in black shrouds
the laws
forbidding me
the world, the truth
under blood oath

forbidding, row upon row
of razors, of statutes
of molars, of grinders—

those bloodshot eyes
legal, sleepless, maneating

—not letting me
not
let blood

GRIMSLEY, MAGISTRATE

Like a grey faced
god almighty, fallen

in decrepitude,
the judge
doles out days in purgatory.
Pity him.
These fresh faced
virtuous lawbreakers
tear him apart.
Marauding, merciless
they plant a bomb
in his vitals, like a bomb
in a briefcase, then snapped shut.
One of these days
like a shot black bird
he will fly, fly apart.

IN JAIL WE HAD A GLIMPSE OF THE SKY

Majestic, undefiled
clouds lord it overhead—
out of sight, out of mind

and who are we   and who are we?

In nature's lexicon
of reason and unreason—
in the mind's store
of wisdom and mad omission

what abides   what abides?
Great spirit, greater reason.

The root has touched rock.
We abide. We abide.

ZEN SHOVEL

we dug a grave
on the white house lawn

The fuzz were furious
dragged us away

But the little shovel
an industrious angel
went on digging
to judgment day

Down down it dug
and down and down
Up up it piled
that bloody spoils

And the angel whispered
to my puzzled soul
The further you dig
into origins
the deeper deeper
origins get.

HOMECOMING

Came home from jail
(wings clipped, spirit subdued)
stood at the threshold
a long time gazing;

The greenery, well watered
blazed like a bush of noon.
Stood there
a sack of bones, inanimate, all eyes.
Tears started in an arid face.
Too sudden the passage—
an experiment in hell—to
modest paradise.

IROQUOIS

Every morning I put on the skin of my feet
and set out for the trading post

where my life gets cheated.
I barter time for combustion
and burn on my feets' skin
like a torch
or a human oven

Every morning I put on the skin of my eyes;
struck blind on the spot
as a stone underfoot
or a foot upon stone
I grope and cry like a gospel
where, where is my healer?

Every morning I put on the skin of my teeth
and grind my teeth
like a mad millstone
an exhausted prisoner still
in Danbury pen, in the dental clinic
where the prisoners show like dogs their teeth
to the guards and owners
who barter dogs
for combustion, for blindness
for stones underfoot—
he carcases of dogs
their teeth and bones and hair—

AND I MAKE IT
I make it
home to evening, home to my soul
my place, my moon and stars

by the skin of my teeth

GEORGETOWN POEMS (1)

One Thinks Of Friends In Trouble Elsewhere, Or; Change The Regime But Keep The Prisoners By All Means

The new political prisoners were given the task
of whitewashing the walls of the cells

polluted, pockmarked by the despair
of political prisoners of the old regime.
The same cells, it goes without saying.

The new political prisoners were given the choice
of whitewashing the slogans of the old regime
of preparing the ideology of the new regime
or residing indefinitely in the whitewashed cells
of political prisoners of the old regime—
the same cells, it goes without saying.

The lies were different, it goes without saying
until you examined them; then they were the same.
The prisoners were different, it goes without saying
until you examined them; infected wounds,
malnourishment, broken jaws; then they were the same.

The cells were different, whitewashed
odorless, it goes without saying—

until the new political prisoners scratched their coda
with bloody fingernails, and found
like a buried city or the cry of walled in prisoners—
the lives, the torture, the outcome
were the same
like the fingers that make a word
and the fingers that make a word
(yours, that blood brother
named you)

in two sides of a crazy mirror.

GEORGETOWN POEMS (2)

Two A.M. And All's Well

Every night the poet opens the gospel
because

(he begs you, understand his plight)
he's a fool
and drinks unceasingly
at that fountainhead of fools.

He drinks and is rendered
like Hyde to Jekyll
like a cork soul impaled on a corkscrew

unrehabilitatable

GEORGETOWN POEMS (3)

I Hope And Pray This Doesn't Happen To Me

When the poet recanted
they hacked off his fingers
and gave him a signet ring

The poet recanted.
They tore out his tongue
and crowned him their laureate

He was then required
to flay himself alive;
two houses of congress
applauded, they dressed him
in the Aztec cloak of immortals

The poet surrendered his soul
a bird of paradise
on a tray of silver held
in his two hands

His soul flew away;
the poet
by prior instruction
vanished where he stood.

GEORGETOWN POEMS (4)

On Being Asked to Debate H. Kissinger

When I sat down
they said with relief,
He's sat down at last.
But I hadn't. I was off like a shot put
and over their walls.

When I grew silent they said,
We've convinced him at last.
But they hadn't. I beckoned my soul aside
Come! pick apples, feed on your vision.

Then I stopped breathing.
They said in relief,
We can breathe again in the world
and deceive with virtuous tongues
and kill with immaculate hands.

And they could, they could. Except
for these lines, those apples, that vision.

GEORGETOWN POEMS (5)

Thank You, Your Point of View Is Certainly Interesting, If Somewhat Bizarre. Are There Any Questions?

The suburbs are sad as death
the university slumps on its arse
money dreaming of money.
Washington DC, a whitewashed sepulchre
awaits the diggers of history
side by side, tombs, slums, imperial empathy.

Amid all this
the transfixed tourists
the international pimps

the wheelers and dealers
rolling along like chariot wheels of fate
the faces like faces on dollars—

amid all this
did one original mind
cry out a gospel verse

panic in the streets!
tumbling whirlwinds!
the unbearable halo
of resurrected Christ!

GEORGETOWN POEMS (6)

Wherein Are Explained My Reasons For Going From The University To The Pentagon, And Breaking The Law, Georgetown Having Accepted Gross Millions From The Tyrant.

Because I don't want to look like the nose of the shah.

Because I don't want to look like the lapdog of the shah's
sister.

Because I don't want to look like a serpent's tooth.

Because I don't want to look like a bureaucrat's belly
stuffed with hunting licenses.

Because I don't want to look like the whites of the eyes
of the dead, or a flag of truce.

Because I don't want to look like an odorless armpit,
or a war on dirt, or a born again briefcase.

Because I don't want to look like an abortionist's pail
or a bishop's crook
or a crooked bishop.

Because I don't want to look like a bloody gag
Exhibit No. 27653 In The Matter Of The Crime Of Silence.

GEORGETOWN POEMS (7)

The Trouble With Our State

The trouble with our state
was not civil disobedience
which in any case was hesitant and rare

Civil disobedience was rare as kidney stone
No, rarer; it was disappearing like immigrants' disease

You've heard of a war on cancer?
There is no war like the plague of media
There is no war like routine
There is no war like 3 square meals
There is no war like a prevailing wind

It blows softly; whispers
don't rock the boat!
the sails obey, the ship of state rolls on.

The trouble with our state
—we learned it only afterward
when the dead resembled the living who resembled the dead
and civil virtue shone like paint on tin
and tin citizens and tin soldiers marched to the common whip

—our trouble
the trouble with our state
with our state of soul
our state of seige—
was
Civil
obedience

THERE'S AN EIGHTH DAY COMING

(for my friends, the poets of Maine State Prison)

Watch the barred sunrise
watch the barred sunset
and in between
weepalong   weepalong

The palms of the hands of the dead
sweat   The eyes of the dead
are impaled
on the bars of the sunrise
the bars of the sunset

Tell them a poem!
the unrehabilitated
dead   like mocking birds
blinded by moonlight
sing back to you!

SOMEWHERE IN THE MIDDLE

My life goes like this.
The Christians decided to make a Jew of me.
I ended up around someone's neck
an albatross or crucifix
anyway, a 'saving metaphor'.
Never a glimpse of the author's
sour sweet face, though his heart
hammered away—
Providence, you're providential!
That way I hung in there, hanged.

And the Jews?
When I came around, they laid it down hard;
love us, love yeretz Israel!
When I stammered out

certain distinctions between
the blood stained faces and the blood stained earth
they'd have none of it, fists came down.

So
my destiny (big deal) is
marginal as a cockroach or a crucifix.
I wander the strait and narrow

Broadway; among the stupefied and stoned
the mutterers and mugged
hanging on like the tails of kites
to mad time and its drovers, up wind and down
Broadway, the ravenous kites, trucks, trailers—

I'll add this; if you sought me
you'd find me
cross hatch in the narrow strip
between cross draughts of hell
cross legged on a filthy bench
forever, next to nothing.
Like a lotus there, or a sunrise—
you've never seen on the Big Apple, such a smile.

FOR THE VIETNAMESE CHILDREN WHO PERISHED ON A FLIGHT FROM SAIGON, APRIL 1975

Having no tears like
having no money

O where replenish
the springs of my eyes?

the children ring me round
tin cups in hand

clamoring

you steal our blood
to make your bread

you spin us blindfold
in a game   you great ones

it's like death   except
for death, they weep—

but for us
no one knows
no one
knows
no
one
knows

FOR FRIDA

The virtuous life, little child
is called by the wise, the great *tao.*
They say; when the belt fits
the belly is forgotten.
When the shoe fits
the foot is forgotten
when the truth impels
the mind is forgotten.
They advise
(bringing the mystagogues to earth with a thump)
when hungry, eat
when weary, lie down.

It is beyond doubt presumptuous
to amend such holy witness.

Still, think of this;
the trees, those inoffensive
Buddhist beings, are rooted in blood

their blossoms drop blood, their fruits
stain the mouth

Such horror
suggests a contrary logic;

in fasting, vigiling, go counter to the illusory
stampede of well being.
The bodhisattva is neither stuprous nor sleek
he is crucified.

16. Block Island

THE SEA shadows itself, surf like thought
crosses a boundless brow.
The house arose, to look the sea in eye.
Slowly it arose, a child surprised
in a world such—wind, wet, battering storms,
then sun and calm
every mood in the lexicon
and the house enduring, a child required
by harsh stricture, to grow strong suddenly.

#

Then came friends for healing respite
out of the city's iron clutch
the desperate amenities
of Burial Brigade.
The names kept on the wall
like a votive wall
or a litany of linked loves.
You know them as do I
by heart: scholars, cooks, poets
meditators, for whom sea & land
are one blessing, like the paste
of spit and dirt, an unguent
in the Healer's hand.

#

House took a chance, as Christian dwellings must
against odds enduring. Weathers opposed
and defects, through which like soul or air
the essence leaked of house.
That was the first delict, from date of birth.
The sea eyed it closely, a gorgon the newborn,
an appetite
a succulent morsel.
Muttered, king of the beasts: I'll inch toward it
I'll have the cliff for first course.

#

Signed, sealed, delivered
my letter to the world
half blotted by sea wind
those surrogate tears
written here, sealed here—
the skin-thin envelope of these walls!
An urban dray horse
out of harness, I was
in my own eyes, next to nothing.
Here I resolved: Be next to
nothing! Shortly
a galling wound healed.

#

The nearest a Jesuit knows
of dwelling place. Caravanserai, long house,
urban rooms paid through the nose, shimmy here
shunt there.
Here, sea, land, sky conjoint: with evening fire
Greek quaternity, reality!

#

'It's not making friends
is difficult, but keeping them,'
my father intoned, correct
after the fact, and in person
unverified. Keeping of friends
keeping of house,
learned hardly, late, in pain.
Was it death taught us
drawing us hand in chalky hand
around the hearth, around the bier
processionally?
Lesson 1: in silence
bread rises. 2: sour tongues

spoil the sauce.
3: learn the art
dismiss the dodge; eyes must meet
if friends are not to
turn back, turn away, turn sour.

#

Island too small for continental egos; continent too vast
for island souls. I say our souls are islands
contrary to John Donne. We bump and touch
like boats with blind eyes. Crowds
contaminate; not wilfully, in necessity, condemned.
I summon compassion,
the undefeated faces of the subway run
wishing them solitude, this house, cliff,
wild roses, blackberries, scoured pines
the panoply, the subtle dance
self's truth emerging like a headland
when morning fog uplifts a seventh veil.

#

Day in, day out
I sought a unifying theme, sought without knowing.
The little house
all eyes, saw for me. I peered through windows
that colored nothing dank or rosy, saw
a waxy bush billowing like a sail; or hunched
face downward, a buffalo riding storm.
No. A mere bush, no burning bush.
Humbled, thankful, hereby I name it.

#

Memories. Guests at table
noble friends, twice ennobled by death
they sup, depart—
transfigured, undefiled,

down cliffside, turn in farewell.
We saw or thought we saw
them
walking sea waves
away, away, into dawn.

#

Life, death, friendship,
thoughtful and bantering converse,
the house read our thoughts, or thought to,
grew wise before its time. Seasons,
succession of birds; in eaves
like overhanging brows, singing bees,
emblems of survival.

#

I am of age when grief
is measured by the hollow beat
of shinbones (mine)
against thin-skinned time.
Who dies, and I do not?
Who dies, and I not granted
in that deep-seated loss, some gain,
another advocate?
Katherine, Anthony, Bertel, Tina,
Frederick, John Leary, Stephen, David,
my own parents—
orate pro nobis.

#

A good house is one
you send love letters from;
itself good news, standing,
withstanding. More to come.

Where then is hope?
not a nail hammered true,
no joist firm without.
Nor could roof sustain
airborne, ceiling bone dry
in driving rain, like spread wing
over fledgling; grace
beyond dumb duty. Fires fare
in face of cold; someone invoked,
someone breathes on behalf.
A large 'meantime' granted against
the world's mad count down. I mean
in all this, hope's many faces.
Then, heart's deep privacy
that keeps and will not tell
fortune, misfortune, all.

#

Go from here, venturesome
knowing not where. A home
is not a tomb. Here Lazarus sleeps
Brief. Then
blazing resurrection.

#

Bill said, 'A gorgeous bird
lighted on the crabapple tree
the day you vanished
trussed, manacled like Odysseus
to mainmast for safe passage.'
(I hope that solo act
was my soul doing its thing;
first, last; in any case
unfettered fervent fling.)

I wander fields nearby
plucking wild sage, mustard, barberry.
And ruminate—
Is this the house
where doubt is exorcised? is this the house
of no betrayal? Our finisterre, the sea
muttering nightlong its witless wild impromptus?
is this the el dorado
of holy fools, who
land failing underfoot
walk water?

#

This house, this house! did not fly flimsy to bits
like cardboard in a chimney flare, at Hiroshima.
No children from this porch fled screaming
their frames, frail kites afire.
Roses bloom
insouciant, vines unimpeded creep the ground
like limbs of fragrant infants.
All, all is noon drenched sweetness
courtesy, reward of sense.
Then that shadow
no larger than a hand
that shadow
crosses, double crosses.
Knowing this
we say farewell, kiss our hand
to house, cliff, island. We give over
elsewhere, our days to stern uses
felonious deeds!

#

Baptized in Christ's death. Water, blood
pour indiscriminate on the little house
which thereupon, like the holy house of Loreto
is rendered fabulous.

Be not astonished
if, on stroke of midnight,
stroke of noon—
table, porch, fundament, roof
pots and pans, with great clatter
levitate in the blue.
Dumb clapboards strike alleluia!
Blue nail heads burn like glass!
Shingles—feathers of birds of paradise!
an angel's shoulder nudges the house, no weightier than
balloon and basket—up, up
into the Presence.

#

Thesis, antithesis, Block Island, Manhattan.
Tomorrow spins the wheel, I spin
into another orbit, friends, frequencies;
the hellish transport's rebellious roar:
sorting mail, like tugging distant nets ashore.
I wish, I wish.
I wish I brought no doubting will
to clear responsibilities
I wish a clearer grace
shone from my face.
Finally that I might give
to those of double will
not reproof, reprieve.

#

Hunger, anger, loneliness.
A gull mews, outcries in noon.
I wonder what he sees, walking high
or does not see. I'd
bargain, a trade off, five minutes;
let him peck away at the mind's machine
while I climb for a look on the wind's ladder.

#

As though
there were future,
as though
there were God.
Two premises
one; predicament, outcome.
This God I never see
until I forget to look
walking the waves, beckoning.
Until I learn to forget
the unbridgeable void between
that One and me—
I a land creature
can have no hope.

#

America. If fame evades it's because
you're probably unamerican.
Fame: sludge at the bottom of the wine cup.
I want to be famous
only as this house is
to ten or twelve friends
who breathe in its skin;
from its eyes
see on a windy day
an old NY Times dismembered
tumble head over heels away.

#

Something. More.
Now and again heard
in uttermost silence
voice of a summoning bird
tipping the world to innocence.
Gospel moments.
We dwell outside the wall
exiles, without maps.

#

Rare spirit, rare,
Harvard College had not his peer.
'An award for drowning do gooders,' he joked
when honors came his way.
Now a face shines
on water, as though an angel
shone momentary there. And we weep,
letting go.
Memory, keep him,
memory, never the less.
Summon in bread and wine
primary acts. The Lord's death
barely to be borne—
must be, must be. That necessity
I take for discipline, a bell rope
ringing changes, fast, furious
must be! must be! in dead hands.

#

Imagine John Leary came
seeker and seer to this cottage
before the world broke
his untameable heart.
Imagine his short run
ended
at this land's end.
Murmuring his Jesus prayer
at last he knew
all that is knowable
though the world's brutish will
break like sticks or bones
noblest hearts first.
At wit's end, at such ending
of promise, sweetness, surmise
fantasy takes hold—
John Leary at cliff side
life's headlong venture
by no means stalled.

John Leary, child
of air, earth, fire—
his Jesus prayer
come true at last, vision
consumes belief like a straw.
In his element at last
he follows the walker of waves.

#

Yesterday, unutterable
island tragedy.
Two little boys at play
climbed in, slammed the door
of an abandoned ice box
in the weedy yard
of a shingled time worn house.
Mother and father scoured
far and near, field and town.
The police chief, the rescue squad
cried the names home: Mike! Danny!
like summoning, in contrary wind
sea waves, tides, drowned lambs.
No avail.
Propped in one small box
surrounded on autumn hills
by three hundred islanders, banal death
has its day.
The Baptist minister weeps
invoking numina of faith
mothers, merchants, sailors, stevedores
sway like reeds
in rude storm.

#

Once on a time, children perished
otherwise—spectacular at sea
or tumbled over monstrous cliffs

or by witch's wiles brought low—
seized by the great fist of fate
that savage sibyl, that claw and claimant,
that hand from a muttering cloud.
No more. It is junk yard death
rusty death
death the recusant, the coward
the undoer of children.
No legend accrues
as of plagues, dervishes, ghosts at dawn
cities evaporated
torturers racking the human frame
stretching the soul's measure.
No. Craven weak kneed death
death the cliché, literal toothy death
let us amid tears, despise.

At the childrens' funeral
women wept free, men
like camoulage of mourners
stood stiff among the stones
(for honor, for balls, for America)
One gesture redeems all!
The young mother, tragic, bowed
like a grandmother crone
(that hour's pitiless blow)
placed a rose on the white box,
a wraith, withdrew.
Then all were summarily dispersed
by a silk suited official face.
The rose, the box, ourselves
suspended
in mid air, mid gesture
amid the mounds of
dead mortician grasses.
And the dead children
not yet dismissed

lay like dreamers, frozen in dream
in surmise, in limbo, in tears withheld.
Then in vision, I tossed a great dark clod
upon their prison. Dust
to dust! I yelled. And the children
laughing, mounted
dolphins
bounding
elsewhere.

#

It wasn't striving
counted for much, it was
play, interplay, dovetailing;
The gulls' cake walk & take off
achieving with minimal brain power
marvels of grace. Aloft, the birds walk
like God intoxicated ghosts
an extra gospel mile,
winds' graceless rebuff
not rebuffed in turn
but beckoned, welcomed, packed in!
Wings hunched, birds put on the wind
like sleeves of gown or great coat
Then roll the wind
like a newspaper under arm
carried home.
Home. Believe it, good news!

#

17. Hymn to the New Humanity

Hymn to the New Humanity

(Nicaragua, El Salvador, and the U.S. June, 1984)

The guns are common as stacked firewood, and as cheap.
They are common as walking sticks carried by the aged and infirm.
There is a gun for every contra who carries a gun.
There are toy guns for infants and flowery guns for little girls.
To the delight of children, there are clown guns that go !popopop!—and wouldn't harm an insect.
There are chocolate guns for Easter; guns that spout water and guns that sprout a parasol for rainy days.
The guns of course have eyes. The guns of the Guardia Civil have ears. And there are merchant guns that smell a dollar, like a miser's nose in a sirocco of money.
And statesmen's guns, equipped with silencers, sheathed like their owners in raw silk, a spiffy outfit.

There is a rare gun, a gun of dark rumor. The ultimate gun, the gun named god. Like god, it has never been seen; in virtue of the invisibility, it must be believed in.
Somewhere, no one knows where, whether on land or sea or in the air, this gun is sequestered, stroked, nourished by the hands of servitors.
Like the queen bee of hell, it waxes in the dark; fed on morsels of children, boiled eyes and pickled ears. It is indifferently a carnivore, a florivore, a faunivore.
This is a metaphysical gun. It renders all other guns, together with their makers and users, redundant.
It is aimed at the heart of history, the secret wellsprings of life.

Innocent as the three famous monkeys, guns see no evil, speak no evil.
Guns believe in guns, guns hope in guns, guns adore guns. In the new dispensation, these are honored as theological virtues.
There are loving marital guns. They vow fidelity, each to the other, at the altar of revolution. Thereupon they are blessed by clerical guns in white surplices.
Also guns are laid on the table at Mass, next to the bread and wine; then they are said to be consecrated guns.
There are guns held by sheep and guns held by goats. To the former

Christ says: Come ye blessed. To the others: Depart from me. Or so it is said.

In El Salvador, the guardia peer out from behind the smoked windows of vans, like Mississippi sheriffs behind their shades; the look of a leveled gun.

In Nicaragua, the guns have learned to smile; like cornucopias of metal, they whisper promises: Dear children, trust us; from our barrels pour the *ABC's*, medicines, a blessed life. Trust us, stroke us, vote for us. In our dark void is concealed all your future.

It has proved embarrassing on occasion that the Christian documents are recusant on this matter of guns. Exegetes, artists, poets, intellectuals have been moved in consequence, to create as it were, a contrary hypothesis. The empty-handed Christ, they declare, "would have," "must have," "might have"

carried a gun. Or at the least, he favored their legitimate use; just guns for just causes.

In the older iconography, the hands of Christ are by no means empty. They bear the bounteous fruit of a storied imagination: shepherd's staff, teacher's scroll, a lamb or two, wheat, chalice. Now these sublime and simple things are lifted from his hands. Even that bloody heart, livid as a skinned plum, to which his index pointed as a very *sigillum* of love—it is torn from his side.

We have in fact imagined a better way of imagining him than he was capable of.

What has occurred is roughly this. There came a time when it was no longer possible to venerate the older symbols of the holy and human. Our species evolved, in accord with exigencies of time and place.

A new human emerged from the tired womb of tradition; a tradition which here and there, through service of lip and heart, had preached a cult of—gunlessness.

A gauche ideology indeed! On its behalf, believers failed to coin a usable term. Nonviolence? It was a clumsy transliteration. They were gunless, that is all.

Our own times signaled a breakthrough. Guns were no longer mere instruments of bleak choice. They were now simply a matter of wholeness, morphology. To this point, to be born gunless corresponded, in the ethical sphere, to a mishap in nature; an armless or legless or sightless being; one lacking in a substantial component of the human.

Thus, to bring a long matter around, a fresh light is cast on a very old subject.

Meantime, it must be admitted that a few recalcitrant priests and their *sequaces* spurned the light. In public places they intemperately cried out the old credo to their gunless god. They were dealt with, summarily.

Our genetic leap postulated a new ikon. The older images had died with their god. They were best buried, once for all.

In this matter we were relentless: new humans, a new god.

Our theology produced a generation, not of iconoclasts, but of inspired entrepreneurs. We now possess, in plazas and shadowy corners, in discourse and dance, the Christ we have come so richly to deserve.

18. The Mission

APOLOGIA

Came an offer, cutting a four-month slice
out of my whole-grain life.
Would I voyage to the Colombian jungle, the Argentine waters,
to advise and consent (to differ, raise mild hell)
in uneasy consonance,
to assemble a scattered myth
the bare bones of the heroic dead?

Who could tell if spirit escaped
split skulls, rent bodies, tempest and travail
to haunt our history, advise, consent, raise holy hell
in the misspent, misshapen world,
edgy, sputtering, intent on dealing
the knockout blow

to the Mount of Blessing
and the Man of the Mountain,
to the Maker and Walker of waves
to the pearl of price
the plenteous harvest
the groaning table
of the Kingdom banquet.

Therefore came. Would have the pearl
agleam in the mind
and the prodigal boy
in tears reconciled
and the wretch by the road
unaccountably succored.

and Jesus the weaver
of chansons de geste
undisplaced by dissonant
artisans of ruin.
Jesus striking
like a blind harper
the song of thc end

who sees in the dark
of days, the light.

The heroic dead.
A vagrant hint, a gleam of spirit,
a playful beckoning; why not come?

Therefore came.
Steep, steep the way.
Pursue the gleam. The story half told
foretold. And over and over
and again and again.
And no way out.
And "I am the way."

HOW THE MISSION CAME TO BE

Someone raked in a veritable World Bank of pesos, and
brought the impossible to pass—
The crossing of continents and their intervening seas
was done in a Rash.

Costumes from Italy, hundreds of wigs descending on sensible
and daffy heads.
And the food! shrimp in the jungle and ice-cream cones for
children and the childish and their dads.

Class distinctions honored like ten commandments at
a punctilious port royal—
Actors dined with actors, workers sat on their hands,
Colombians perched like parrots on the lowest rung of all.

A fiesta! spectacles and astonishing stunts by
night and day,
The Indians swam the air like fireflies, the altitudinous stars
said their silvery say.

And the pesos fell, a tropical rain, a Holy Spirited British
Protestant sign—
predestination or some such, under the camera's omnivorous
eye.

Then the canisters rolled like wheels of Ezekiel, heavy with
auguries across the seas
Rolled up jungle and ocean and bird calls and tarantulas,
in short, all of us.

Life was a lark in Eden (except for spiders and serpents,
except for the rumor, the wrong jump, the odd pratfall)—
Time catapulted, world syncopated; a ripe mango in a
shaken orchard. Immortality is all!

A VISIT TO THE ONANI INDIANS

You dwell lifelong in a jungle clearing
A hut; a plank porch, yourself, and
the vast gangrenous green, proliferating
far as the encircled eyes' round.
Then you'd better create poetry!

It's plain survival!
(An Indian, a prisoner knows)
Like a plumed sun in high style
You sway, pound the earth in praise;
Your paint proclaiming wilful bodily joy
and the drums speak for you, the flutes.
O the dance, the heart set free

the vowels of birds in vocal reed,
the body's splendor,
the momentary lost and found
blaze of the human!

TO SAINT PETER CLAVER

I.

Heal us Jesuits; the overly content, the malcontent,
the skilled and sere of heart, the secret weepers,
the self-defeated, the defaulters, the proud of place
drinking the empty wind of honor. Help the workhorses
slow, speed the laggards, give back to routine and rote
their lost soul.
Institution, constitution, order, law—O
kiss the dead awake!
Your holy Spirit, come!

II.

(on leaving Cartagena, 1985)

The noble dead lie in unmarked graves
countless in my generation,
known only to God, who moulds faces
with potter's thumb, wheel, and treadle,
then, holds the broken dead like a lover
weeping for the wrecked work.

Harmless, pretentious as puff pigeons
the generals, their war-horses, their public faces
prance in midair, going
nowhere. Their war cries pollute public places.

A town at war, soldiers
led to slaughter
march through public places
baa-baaing like sheep.
Preternatural their tears
their noble mockery and mime.
Known only to God, they fall in Unknown places.

At San Pedro Claver, the saint reposes
"Slave of the slaves," his self-entitlement and glory

a lamp of apocalypse in the bridegroom's hand.
Outside, beggars, cripples hover
apocalyptic spirits of earth and air,
purgatorial bodies and souls
(could we but read not run, like blinded sheep baa-baaing!)

In the public place, a general, his war-horse,
fused gargoyles, pour their mad
molten rhetoric, mad trumpets blare
on the innocent air.

The saint turns to rest, an unextinguished lamp, his tongue
foresworn to silence before mad Pilate,
the absurd stick sword,
the bronze bluff of imperium melting like wax or flesh.

Silence, innocence, soul, sweet revenge
of truth outraged
O might the slaughter-bound sheep
flock to this well of life,
draw from the throat of the dead
than "baa-baa, pity the death-bound
sheep in sheep's clothing!"—
a mightier work and word!

Pray; sheep cast off their fleece,
mutton and muddle. The general
pluck from his breast the brassy clock
tick-tocking doom on doom,
cast it in the blaze
the saint in his combustible body lit, a
watchman's fire on Cartagena's walls.

UNBORN

The National Park gave on the sea
that fought to a frenzied impasse.

The land countered, set a warrior's shoulder
so cut its losses.

We entered; a crude lettered board:
THIS LAND BELONGS TO THE COLOMBIAN PEOPLE
SOME OF WHOM ARE DEAD
SOME LIVING
BUT MOST ARE UNBORN.

We trod warily
as though on All Souls' Night,
parting the vines
thick as warriors' wrists—

Borrowers, ancestors, heirs
in a land not ours.
The unborn, the dead
a cloud of witnesses
around, overhead.

BECAUSE

On the Don Diego
the dugouts assemble
like a sublime children's charade:
"By River, Indians and Jesuits Enter the Mission."
In my hands
a leather-bound volume:
"Summa Theologica, Venice, 1773."
I sit awash.
The vast tome opens like the throat of a sage
to "Article Eighty-four:
Wherein Are Adduced Five Reasons
Why God Is Named Love."
(In quaint Latin) "Because God is source
of love, because
God creates for love, because
God would have us love as we are loved,

because"—I raise my eyes,
the multifarious jungle leaves astir—
an open volume
grown voluble, uttering
reasons beyond number, for
love beyond reason.

SO WE PASS

The Jesuit robes swath us, who shall be
like those originals, bones stacked and sacked
by vandalous time, sifted in God's great
hourglass upended. So we pass

as they did
into God's holy Son—
the Pardoner, his temporal flesh
vandalously, too, undone.

I touch the fabric; it rots. So time
touches me. I become
less bodily, like the sun
rising upon its light; more like the Son
as brother is belike. And heart
quickens its beat; entrance rite
into—believe it—being.

MYTH

Uncertain we were
whether parable and fact were one.
River and ocean made together
marriage processional,
mystic joining of hands.
The Don Diego curved like a bent bow,
shot us under summoning drums
into full sight and majesty.

The mythic being
received, like arms to breast
time, river, ourselves riding time and river—
into, we knew and knew not
what—the vast sun-reddened
artery of all.

THE CLIMB

Descending laboriously
the lost mountain village
round, round the cone our travail,
tracing a rune on the wild secret face.
We heard the sea
then lost the sea
then saw it face to face—
delight of sense, loss of delight.
Not yet not yet
in exhausted end
to see and hear and taste. O more to
swim in beatitude.

ANNIVERSARY

Hiroshima Day. I remember
at Iguaçu the waterfall, a moveable
unmoving feast for the eye.
Gigantic, thunderous, proclaiming
the glory of God, the advent of
hierophants of the last hour.
Not warriors; witnesses
standing watch perpetually
as the world pitches over, a suicide.
Or angels, and the tomb's mouth
empty of death, a house of honeycomb.

THE LIGHT YOKE

We clambered upward in jungle mud,
fell flat, stood once more.
Cold, cold as the waters
that drenched us with green hell.
Jeremy gasped, "What men they were,
those Jesuits
who dared it first, no all-seeing eye
publishing them to the world."
Yes, but no world
hectoring them either.
No Nicaragua
raining its fall of blood on their backs.
Only calabashes, hammocks, cases,
and the light yoke of the Gospel.
Then the mickmockery of macaws
scrambling the plain command—
The harsh and dreadful word called love.

WAITING

I've waited a long time
in and out of jungles
for I know not what—
"That this mortal body
put on immortality?"

We wore the shabby moth-eaten robes
that so resemble the body, its wear and tear.
I said, "This might be the cassock
I entered the Jesuits in."
Now it most resembles
a second aged skin.
And what trump or season
will put it off; and what on earth
will I look like then?

THE WELL

The sweet-water well and the sulphurous world
that soured and wrecked—all, all save this.
Square blocks rise like a round
tower of Atlantis, underwater.
Fearful too; you could pitch over
like an empty bucket, fill to brim, sink,
a stone in a dark pocket.
Deep, deep as God's
first thought of God.
Someone cast a round mirror
down and down
where things begin to be.
Faces leapt back at me,
masks, memories, angels on guard,
tender advocacies and vows,
skies broken by thunderous hammers,
days long vanished into enchantment's cave,
auras, lives loved, lost at last.
Everything, nothing.
It was airy water after watery air.
"Come down, come down,"
the mirror whispered.
"I promise (cross
my false heart)—
beatitude.
Kiss me
and drown."

WATERFALL

We disappear under the waterfall
as though in time. The water falls and falls;
true time
in disaccord, warped; past, always past,
a trick named time. The waterfall calls

like a truthful angel, true time,
the poetry of things; no slack prose
(things as they are, we as we are).
The angel commands. We disappear
under the waterfall. Emerge
drenched in beatitude;
no actors, no additional souls—
agents, conquerors, walkers of water!

HEROES

They've seven dummies of a "crucified Jesuit"
to toss over the falls. I saw them tumble
like cheerful ships, arms soaring, oaring.
One, headlong like a champion, thirsting
for the finish. Another, feet braced
loomed vertical at the brink; a momentous
Nijinsky leap. "Farewell," he intoned,
a priest red as sunset.

Thus goes the film. Not thus life
which alas, tosses real meat to surreal
dogs. No contest. The falls
named "Devil's Throat" are papery
white, a slowly folding envelope, sending
a code word to God; something about
live heroes dying in the jaws
of murderous dogs. And at last, at least
(dogs wreak, gods repair)
an honored immaculate slowly folding shroud.

19. Stations

STATION ONE

The thump of a gavel
("vagrancy   loitering)
JOHN DOE, DEFENDANT
his look   a man condemned
drummed out of the world
That look
ice   fire   bewilderment   despair—
look at him   looking at us!

His crime
No possessions   no property
no equity   no income   no credit
no account
The ultimate affront
(the immaculate myth
the "twin fetishes"   stability   order)
The defendant   hunches forward
not toward the judge
(justice misserved   hopeless)
he knows his fate
thump of gavel   judge   guardian
of who owns what
(of what owns whom)

That look   pierces to the quick

The hammer comes down
Take him away!   away!

Justice must be served
(property must be served
taxes   Caesar)
Take him away!

Nameless   on his way   *via dolorosa*
Where the friends   the disciples?
No one   not one

empty   benches
like graves awaiting   twelve dead men
The judge   lord Pilate
Caesar's right arm   hammer of god
And high above
a stone   throne   cenotaph
on which is graved
The Law!   The Law!

Nevertheless
say it
Today's charge   today's crime
neither vagrancy   loitering   whatever
The crime   speaking clumsily
"propertylessness"

As to our defendant
Behold the man!

How dare he
assault and batter
the above-mentioned
scheme   scam   neat arrangement   dream
Verily   Speedily   Away with him!

STATION NINE

"THIS IS   AN ACCIDENT REPORT
Under Police Barricade   Number 9
a man has fallen
he   or someone very like
reported injured   twice today
elsewhere   in the city"
(The staccato voice
crackling with tension   urgency)

"Identity unknown"
(identity too well known
homeless   John Doe)

Naming   being named
act   of biblical import—
at dawn of creation
a noble task   laid upon humans—
to "name all things"
Names infer   confer   vocation
Isaac   Daniel   Ezekiel   Jesus
The third fall
the stairs rise   straight up
tidal wave   nightmare
hydra-headed   pummeling
He lies there   hapless   helpless

This fallen one
We pause
we read   a larger meaning
indeed the name
Homeless J. D.
something   communal   tribal
"We have not here
a lasting dwelling"

And if perchance   supposing   otherwise
We wheel and deal   connive   compel
Consuming   self-consumed—
solely intent on
"the things which are seen"—
we stand self-deceived

"Dwellers upon the earth"
dwellers   nowhere else
no hope   no soaring   no breakthrough
slaves drawing water   indentured
to the wheel of time

We pause
upon this fallen one
mortality   stasis
recumbent   bloody

Vital signs all but extinguished
Yet
he will stand again
walk again
The end is not yet

We do not know the end
and we know
He does not know the end
and He knows
Mind spins about
somewhere between
noble fiction
and sorry fact
Homeless J. D.
and homeless J. C.—
the Son of Man
"had not whereon
to lay His head"—
One day His last
He fell to earth
and twice and thrice
Nevertheless
went on went on
to consequence
We hardly dare name it—
a borrowed grave—
all said worst done—
Then
dawn burst
day broke
genesis
"He is risen"

A promise nothing more
(hardly less)
cold comfort
under a sorry flimsy marker
Police Barricade Number 9

A sorry   mime of death—
Meantime   all time
the promise   the promise

STATION THIRTEEN

Corner of Thirteenth and Nameless
The nameless one   goes under
who goes there   who lives there
who dies there?
Nameless

and above   and above
blank as God's brow
the hives
where humans dwell   do not dwell
no one to tell   not tell
Empty   boarded   shuttered   window
  after   window
wide-eyed   blank
dead eyes   stare past   the dead
"In my end   is my beginning"
Thus the story   nearly ended
ends
where it began
in the Land of the Blind
(the unafflicted   unaffected   affectionless
passersby   where it began
O you who pass by)

Not all pass by
"Let the little children
come to me   forbid them not"
A street   Thirteenth and Nameless
two waifs
unbidden   unforbidden

Grant the dead   a voice
the living had none

"I inarticulate
spoken for reported on
in death as in life or what passed for life
passive as cobbles underfoot
poked prodded ordered about
disallowed ignored
a statistic on a page
in a file in a drawer
in an office in a building
on a street in a city
any page any file any anyway—
shunted about catalogued kept in place
a 'case' an instance
faceless voiceless
ground under computerized
My passionate soul

"Now the computer
under 'J. D. Homeless'
goes blank buzzes 'dead file'
"Nonetheless
the children come to me
My soul lingers recusant
no sorrow like to my sorrow
I linger
in a blind window
a shell a simulacrum
mockup of life
a curtain waving witlessly
like a flag of truce
in the hands of the dead
'I surrender you win'

"Those children
my parched flesh
grateful astonished—
tenderness unwonted
a tear
springs in the desert"

Street children children of ill luck
child John Doe child Jane Doe
under the ominous
shadow and sign Thirteenth and Nameless
a warning sign a cross-arm
raised like a totem portending
only disaster
"Run from here"
"Linger at risk"

They linger risk
Where did he learn who instructed her
In what hard school Street of Ill Luck?
empty shells blind windows
who the teacher COMPASSION?

"I shall not
altogether die
until I praise
until I kiss my hand
until I place my sorry nimbus
that predilected
vocation of misery
grown glorious
on those dear heads

"Children for this favor
this coverlet laid
tenderly on my
much abused bones—
I swear
by His death and mine
and your and my
trek through hell—
now worn now weary
we shall make merry
in God's great realm"

STATION FOURTEEN

To the city morgue
officials come running
distrait dismayed
wild-eyed stuttering
something going on here
who knows what
nothing of moment
rumors wives' tales

Mors et vita duello
death life in mortal combat

How say it how declare
good news
after bad—
punishment annulled
penalty undone
Someone walks away
victorious
Someone walks toward—
companionable

Finally
(no from the beginning)
I see You
walk toward me
in your wounds
ragtag nameless
J. D. J. C.
those frail speechless bones
alight as a phosphor
that face alight
those wounds

Your credentials—
dying somberly
for others they say

mors et vita   *duello*
then   they say
walking free

walking the cities   walking the ages
what a burden
pondus gloriae   weight of glory—

Tell the litany—
gratitude begrudged
fake and true vows
masses muttered
refusals   reprisals
guns   settling matters
crucifixes   images
graven   groveling
grislier than the event

Then
the "glory gap"—
larger than life   You
begetting less than life
And how measure up
to the measure laid
to the sorry human
mocking   surpassing—
how not dread
mors et vita   *duello*
conflixere   *mirando*
death   life   locked in mortal combat

O give us peace
dona nobis   *pacem*
any peace
any price

Only   in solitude
under heavy crisis
in passing insight

gone   soon as granted—
You come toward me
free   great God free   at last
accretions   fallen away
egos   husks
dead   by the wayside

Can on   befriend   a God?
the question   is inadmissible
Nevertheless
a fiery recognition
lights us—
broken by life
making our comeback

20. In Memoriam

THOMAS MERTON

1. 1969 Opened Like This

I wish I had some joy—
the text of eyes that pay
this year, all the last exacted; tears.
When Merton died, we met, struck dumb,
the old year's locking jaw
let blood, one last time; death, then this death

We blow up big the photo Griffin made—
Kentucky woods, hunched arms
overalls, Picasso moon face. Eyes

like a wrapt stranger among mourners
on a road, of a noon, in a landscape
stinking like graves. Hands outstretched
filled with this world's
(no other's)
flowers, wounds;
I have some joy!

2. At The Time Of His Death, Americans Had Mastered The Dynamics Of A Moon Flight

Merton's gone; that comfort ended.
The moon, bleak as an earth, blinks
bad cess back to us. That comfort
when free as promises or willows
or the future
the moon hung there
and al1 hands lifted
like priests or brides
brides or
(minded and ringed)
geese, straining, crying
a northern tongue—

ended

3. Who's Who At The Obsequies

General Hershey did not mourn
you, nor Roy Harris nor
Cleaver's hell's angels.
The sombre Texan war lord
braved New York crazies
to shed
a vagrant tear
on a cardinal's pall—
he minded this day
his waning power and war.
Et Cetera bought farms
or oxen
or took wives
the day your death
shook the earth's round

Only the raped and rent
the shadowed, submerged
upon whom Kafka's needles
bear down, write large
the cuneiform of loss—

were there. And the four
ministering spirits of these;
earth, water, fire, air.

4. Merton

The years
pouring out
mick & mock & this & that

like a horn of plenty
in the hot hands
of the rich bored

& a friend maybe or even 2
but Christ only
1 you

5. The Funeral Oration As Pronounced By The Compassionate Buddha

Assembled sirs. The courtesies afforded us by the Dali Lama,
the Abbot of the Trappist Fathers
and the vergers of your cathedral, are deeply felt
and enter as a sombre joy into our heart's stream.

The Christ himself (to whom all praise) were better chosen
to speak for this monk, brother and son.
Alas. The absence of your god, decreed by a thousand
malevolencies
susurration, anger, skill in summoning his words against him—
I hear your choice, approving; *one god at a time. Better an*
unknown god, even
a tedious one, than that holy son, native to our flesh.
Better a subtle millennial smile, than anger and infected wounds.
Better me than he. So be it; I shall speak.

The assumption of this monk into ecstasy,
the opening of the crystal portals before that glancing spirit!
He was (I speak a high and rare praise)
not too strenuous after reward; so he attains eternal knowledge.
In his mortal journey, he refused direction from those pylons
impermeable, deadly smooth,
hard to the touch as the membrane of hell.
He detested their claim upon the soul, he exorcised their rumors.

(I too have been a guest in your cities. I have been conducted with
pomp
through your martian workshops, heard with a start of fear
the incantations of your genius.
Indeed the aim is clear; saints, the innocent, visionaries,
all targets of your encompassing death wish.

(But the Buddha knows no disdain; he stoops low to enter your
labyrinth,
to uncoil its secret, to bare its beast.

The Buddha, a length of rope, a dog in the dust; such parables I
embrace
once more, in tribute to this monk.)

The monk has attained god;
he had first attained man. Does the nexus troubIe you, issuing as it
does
from a mouth so neutral, so silent as mine? Be comforted.
Gioconda exists only to smile. She does so; her value mounts and
mounts.

But the monk Merton, in his life and going forth
requires that a blow be dealt
your confident myths. If the gods are silent
if even to this hour, Christ and Buddha stand appalled
before your idols, if we breathe the stench of your hecatombs—
still, the passage of a good man restores;
it brings the gods to earth, even to you!
For once, for a brief space, we walk among you
for a space of words,
we quicken your hearts in pursuit of the sovereign will.
O makers and unmakers! I shall shortly be borne
in a flowering cart of sandal into high heaven; a quaint apotheosis!
The routine slaveries once more possess you.
Man and god, Buddha and Merton, those years, this hour, fold in like
a dough
The blows of the kneading fist withdraw, the times are your own.
War readying of war;
conflicts, games of death, checks and counters—
I leave you, your undoing, promethean doers and despoilers.

Hope?
Christ and Buddha fashion a conundrum. Hear it.
The hour of your despoiling is the hour of our return.

Until then, the world is yours, and you are Moloch's, bound hand
and foot
upon a wheel of fire.

The monk Thomas I take up in lotus hands
to place in the eternal thought
a jewel upon my forehead

WILLIAM STRINGFELLOW

My last death was Stringfellow's.
Death, rattling its begging bowl.
"Sustenance, sympathy!," it whined.

Stringfellow bethought; death
lacking a name
(unnameable, nameless horror,
they mutter in terror)

he named it finally, taming
the appetite that feeds
on kings and clowns
feeds and feeds, never satiated—
women, warriors
the sleepy eyed unborn—
never enough!

"We must break this thrall
once for all" became his mind's
holy obsession and vocation.

Like a priest's crucifix aloft
before the obscene undead—
Christ expiring for love, summoning a last
commanding cry—"Down, dog death!"—

thus Stringfellow—
years and years, crucifix in hand
miraculous he moved in the world
dismaying, dispelling death.

Thus as a sun advances, shadows
go underground.
He stands, believe, in resplendent noon.
Taken from the cross
he ascends straight up.

And death, shadowy, starved, named,
is not
and no where to be seen.

ABRAHAM HESCHEL

(1)

My friend Rabbi Heschel died in sleep.
By day, in sleep. Blessed be G-d.

A cabala. Ponder each phrase minutely.
Over your shoulder
God too reads the text

War killed him, heart stopped in its tracks.
So it was bruited. And wrongly.

That day
he climbed Jacob's ladder, an old man
huffing aloft laborious, until the angels
disemburdened flesh with a kiss
and he joined them
bearded and learned
and light as they.
. . .

(2)

I have nothing of this to keep
but the low rung of a ladder
imagined, not there.
And he saying; Not there, so be it.

Like Someone not there, Creator.

I raise one foot, then another
and a ladder leans to a world
where nothing was. And it is.

ETTY HILLESUM

(d. Auschwitz, Nov. 30, 1943)

"Here goes then," wrote this woman I never heard of.
And "I don't want to be safe, I want to be there."
Wrote this woman.

She is like a God I never heard of.
She is like a bride I never married.
She is like a child I never conceived.
Like death? Death she heard of

death she walked toward, a child lost
in the glowering camps.
After years and years—recognition!

I heard a cry; "My child!"

The ineffaceable likeness. Death
her child, her semblable.
Wrote "In such a world I must kneel. Kneel down.
But before no human." In the furnace
lust and its cleansing, birth and its outcome.
To kneel where the fire burns me, bears me.
Eros, God, Auschwitz.

She wrote; "To live fully
outwardly, inwardly, my desire. But to renounce
reality for reality's sake, inner for outer life—
quite a mistake."

Wrote to her lover; "Dear spoiled man
now I shall put on my splendid dressing gown
and read the bible with you."

O singer of song of songs, O magnificat Mary
O woman at the well of life!

DAVID JOYCE

(a young peacemaker dies on Good Friday)

1.

Stand somewhere! you stood
(cold, cold, placard in hand!
"Thou shall not bomb!"

Lonely, young, steadfast,
tongues of fire warmed you through

and death's paralysis and fix
yielded, and we wintry crept
toward the fire
your pentecostal
crossed
bones
lit

2.

Things useless, frivolous, dear
we brought to your hands—
flowers, sweets, green plants

like offering the panda's dark
vegetarian eye
bamboo shoots, a bribe—

"dear exotic himalayan
visitant, we pray—

do not disdain our hands,
red as hunter's moon, as
Macbeth's drawn blade.
O abide with us, endangered
emblem, guardian, angel!"

3.

At bedside, we read a gospel,
a tale of gentle village healing.
You lay there
eyes closed, tragic believer.
Time and again I hissed like a dervish;
David, be healed!

But the healer
ran for the hills.
was seized,
nailed up, time's trophy

and the hill of skulls
grows on itself, an anti-
miracle spawning
megadeath, mock Easter.

4.

Weeping, nightlong, we rehearsed
the choreography of death.

Two millennia incise
our grief upon an urn

brimming
like time's snowfall

with your sweet dust

5.

Midnight, Good Friday. Jesus
cold as carp on a slab.

David, breathing hard
a runner to the tape—
falls.

Jesus and David dwell in that
crepuscule. No heart stirs
toward life—
the pulse of an egg
near term

cool, not cold.

Warming
toward morning.

6.

A most unamerican life!
no money
no lies
no fear—
soul
like the single note
of a spring-wet willow whistle.
It sounded.
Summoned, he walked.
And of long drawn
wailing at the wall,
nothing.

7.

Augustine mourned his friend;
"dimidium animae meae;
my friend died, half my soul
torn from me."

And David, his larcenous love
runs, runs
through the "selva oscura"

bearing
half my soul in his hands.

8.

The laughing home grown
moustache, the
unutterably clear gaze,
the insouciant shock of hair—
everything improvised,
artless, carefree, noble—

yet
a perfect work
admits of imperfection.
(In hands of
metaphysician Death
prognosis becomes
principle)

at heart,
an infinitesimal
defect
lets
soul
through

9.

I summon   to mind
the flavor and verve of life,
gold through a sieve—
                                        the smile
that moves mountains as clouds move
and are no more.
                                                Wrath too
that strikes east to west, the wrath of God
at the arrow's crime, the falling sparrow.

This I love, summoning you—
"take no thought of tomorrow."

You fit, befit the hand of God—
a silken glove, a sparrow.

10. Finally, A Song Of Songs

We shall see your face again
and the lost pearls
will grace your forehead, grace
the breast of the bride.
The beloved shall touch you
to ice and fire.
You shall know her
and be known.
And both shall sow and both
together reap.

ROBERT SULLIVAN

(murdered by the state of Florida Nov. 30, 1983, with the concurrence of the supreme court.)

1.

I count the heartbeats to the end
I count the breathing to the last
and here, with clash and ceremony comes
a headhunter's banquet
triumphant, borne on a truncheon.
   A still life in my guts, I'll carry it
to ante room, to ante time;
   there, then
   the concatenate powers
periwig, shroud, noose,
the wizened
blank faces, frozen in obduracy—
O appetite, O consummation!

and high above
   perched on the hanging tree,
a scavenger daw

mutters like a mad metronome;
law law law.

2.
(On an airplane, I prayed as he died)

I hover in mid air
among the madly functional
paper chasers, briefcases
while in Starke abbatoir
fervent believers in human
perfectibility, strap you in
blindfold you shave you
plug your ass and nostrils—

then
first strike against
Christ's merciful withheld
great gong of judgment.

Safe neighborhood, safe world!

But the blind flash that makes
smoking meat of informed flesh
and sends soul up a flue—

in bunkers
vats and sea caves
the nukes mutter like hell's hooded
monks in dim stalls—

Dies irae, dies illa.

FOR MY BROTHER, THOMAS BERRIGAN

(R.I.P., August, 1993)

(1)

When the first one died
I said to the others

(my brothers) "look the six
little Indians then were

five!" It was a calculated
clown act,

beleagured grief
flipped on its head.

The sadness, loss

turned up, a grin

and bear it

(2)

What it meant.

The spiffy gabardines
went off in a huff, to other shoulders.
Shoes, laced tight
as space explorers,
took to the four winds.
The shirts like second skins,
elsewhere were fresh, then shoddy.

O what was left him? nothing needful.
One by one, rendered, grim, given over,
he was his bones awhile, blood grown sullen
as a pig pudding. The tongue
that had hymned and cursed us—
nothing; syllables of a book done with.
And the vivid brain
dissolute, then stony.
                                        Not a thought of us
to counter the stone age and its clubs
returning, ravening.

He and we, pure given at the start.
At end
as purely taken,

inexplicable to us
voluble or shaken where we stood.
Declaring as the earth
made a beggar's bowl above him;
Dust to dust. Beyond weighing or worth.

This at first, this all
foreshortened, gone.

What after—
your or my eyesight
or the unblinking appraising
pretender to the throne above,
these—
to his second sight—are next to
nothing.

(3)

First evidence—
a blank, a know nothing
as though all day, a shilly-shally
drizzle drowned the sun, sun
lackluster, blank.
Rain or tears
who knows?
Both.
And the mute landlocked trees
no one walks among
leaves that may be, may not.

C. J. McNASPY, S. J.
(Who died listening to Mozart)

And the light
puts out your eyes.

I don't mean catastrophe
far from it.
Excess of soul
rising like yeast, zest—
(obedient
to sweet exuberance)

is nearer—
the point being,
light.

My notion
leans to a last day, yes
a last breath
a Jesuit death

unexpected, beckoned by
Mozart's right hand
zestful, raising
a signal,

a movement advertent,
birds
rising from earth
as from a dark throat—

your cry
YES YES

and the light
puts out your eyes

JACK ST. GEORGE, S.J.

(R.I.P., November 26, 1993)

1.

Like a candle's eye
we kept watch.

Your death-head face
took from thin air
as from time's instructed ghostly fingers,
final form.

I am waiting
for a mother
for a friend
for the God even we hear of
for the poem
that will bear you off
newborn and bloody
in two arms.

Waiting for tears
for the poem.

Eccolo, death, our everything
our nothing, beats at the door.

And you
cozened, cleansed of blood
propped and readied
for the road, how rocky.

A last kiss
I wanted yours
late,
an alas!
on the wind's blank brow.

2.

Friend
outward sign
of inward grace

I read the sign aright
step within—

the table fitly set

thanks be
body and blood
of star-crossed Christ

and you transfigured
child of my childhood
singing
alleluia
in the upper room
of No Betrayal

3.

Night is centrifuge, it scatters everywhere
night. By day too, awful, and reason of
promise broken and no dawn, more so. Thus
stage is set, for what we know not

as night emboldens, a snake or stream
insinuating indoors, in quest of very soul.

I set this down because you
beyond words, raised
gestures courtly, curt
and singlehanded
a shadowing mountain moved.
You, I saw it, swear it, exorcised
dark, void, calamity.

4.

you
elsewhere bound
of words
no trace

Wait
of a sudden they

flock above, about
like birds
winter bound

No
hear them
sweet, contrary
singing—

"turn turn turn
for it is spring and
you and we and you
have nowhere else"

5.

Pity us
bereft,
no resolution

Who comes
what comes?
a silly street Santa—
ho ho ho
a bell of passing, a plague

the news nothing new—
appetite, obscure murder,
carnivorous famous headliners—
each and all, an obit.

Suppose the worst—
Advent a zero
heaven scatted,

no savior,
nothing worth saving

or maybe
a worst case savior—

not an eyeblink,
and we pleading
Come O come

Still we'd hear
that velvet voice of yours, deep deep
dredging the heart,
or your accordion's grandiose
grin & bear it,
or your tap dance spelling out
a morse code—

The music stops
taps (I lose the metaphor)
yield to the trumpet, taps
the kind we hate
tears and fury and attendant slaughter—
the taps stop short
the toes curl under

It is all one
all said, all done
accordion and code
and Someone

named No One. Hope.

21. Homage to Gerard Manley Hopkins

At the icy gate of horn
you stand and knock.

Such sweetness overtakes
for thought of you, whose thought
like a sleeping child
on banked violets
waking, sees all around
for what it saw
a sweetness more intense.

Eventually you'll unbend
our straightlaced company
that weightily keeps
its so stern enclave, excludes
eye askance,
the pure untrammeled poetry of things

that lurks like a forestalled angel
knocking for entrance
our icy gate of horn.

Angel of poetry

O name us right, lead us
like gospel daughters enchanted
to innocence, sweetness, sacrament

to 'yes,' our Lord.

⋆ ⋆ ⋆ ⋆ ⋆ ⋆ ⋆

I purposed in a poem
sweet in very strangeness
telling what you told, magister—

how in our Christ all things
conjoined, not one escaped
that fowler's, harrier's, gardener's,
mostly, lover''s hand.

Least of all,
last, first, of set purpose, you.

Your longing; trivial life redeemed—
mysterium tremendum, Incarnation.

Tremendum
That God be ignorant from birth? And brawn of youth
clumsy at start,
bent thus and so
to nicety
of joist and notch and beam?

Tremendum
infused with trivial—
a mewling infant
essays a first step, molds sounds
tantamount to words, grows confident.
An unsubmissive gaze at length
sizes the world,
finds to his eye, little at home
wanting, much alas abroad—
dire lack,
illest luck.

And blesses, curses, draws
with heal-all skill,
ill humors up from root.

And crafts his stories
pinking the adversaries' sham and shame.

Is ringed about and baited,
false kissed is taken, hanged.

'Done with him!'
such breath of relief
raced
like slippery rumor through the world.

Stopped short.

Someone sped, faster than ill wind.
A ghostly fist beat at the door
A revenant
back (He said, who stood there
pointing the road He came)
back from the dead.

Or here or there, who knows,
breaking bread withindoors,
showed for proof
such wounds as scar the living never.

In you and me
Himself discovers, in
mirrors of disbelief
and belief
we hold to him, flashing
our clashing signals, souls.

Look too, He holds
and loses hold of
and plucks from thin air safe
the swooping mad bird, hope.

Thus do great events and puny
mingle, make in total
mysterium tremendum, both.

Of us, take it for this—
a father hoisting a child
aloft, confers
horizon, scope, command.

The little one
owns all he surveys, all.

A prelude shakes him, head to foot.
Lord Nonce, he
gestures grandly;
                    'Why
it is all mine! his stride
serves for my own! what he is
surely I shall be!

★ ★ ★ ★ ★ ★ ★

In the matter of love instruct us, poet.
Out of excess, out of lame and lack
we choose,
lackluster, excessive
—badly, badly.

Speak of what transpired
in field, cross road, portal, town,
when a hand
lay on afflicted flesh

and shortly
(as when in still waters
carefree, a stone is cast)
the common shambles
grew a great space
for dance, for song, for sight of
(O blind, mute, halt, no more!)
sunrise's swift glory.

A poem—
bulwark, raised hand against
onslaught of death

Not that we fear death
(so you insistent
and plaintive sang).
We fear God most justly
and in fear stands our dignity.

Does God not stand in dignity
fearful of us?

You saw
wreckage incipient
and trembling, wept.

Worse nears.
The days mark us
like timber for the ax.

We tremble hearing
the fierce reverberating grief of earth
as round and nearer,
soundless, anonymous,
whole forests fall.

* * * * * * *

The being you saw,
a windhovering bird,
a savior set free—

chevalier, dauphin
Christ our Lord—

death downed, like a moon
when sun makes day.

* * * * * * *

What you took seriously
(*Therefore*,
a bronze hinge
opened majestically)
—stars, springtime,
a candle indoors,
kingfishers,
dragonflies,
all beseeching
'O speak for us!'—

you laid on each
the strange searching stigma of imagination.
The achieve of, the mastery
who knows how? stands.

★ ★ ★ ★ ★ ★ ★

In you Gerard, in a few
others I see
the 'instress' of Jesuits

essence
soul of soul, yes
Christ, stupendous 'instress'
of multitudinous being,
from whose brow was wrung
the thorny
thought of us—

the 'thisness'
that lent you like a bush
afire, a phoenix intensity

(the form, the fiery, firm
purpose forever thwarted
beyond your best
to invoke, desire, in truth
to serve and be served by!)

Well,
we dwell if we but knew it
somewhere along the spectrum
'human,'
to be or become

insinuated like a thread
into creation's warp.
The law you followed—
'form following fire'—

passion of being, to be
passionately underscored,
no other invading
the precinct 'haecceitas'—

Yes.

Baptised by the gracious raised
shell of your spectral hand,
I see with a wiser eye,
follow the rove and rhythm

your touch bestowing
like lustral waters
lush, large,
            reality.

* * * * * * *

Dwelling long among your themes
praise, I think
becomes you most. *Kenosis* of self
breaking the cup,
repairs, fills it the more, that Other.

Splendors press,
lowly things linger—
fishes, finches,
stones, bells, tucks of string—
creatures of upper air,
near nothings.

Then to the leap, *the just man justices.*

Who in mind's eye
strung them, what theme
hung them, a necklace
about Christ?

It was a feat
nice to nuance and substance.
The poet, disclaiming praise
heaping it high, hymning
that beloved Other
only
owns it the more.

★ ★ ★ ★ ★ ★ ★

Taking stock of
such as myself—

and enduring as I must
the dark quandary
named here, named now—

until a knell sound
and the sea gives up its dead
and continents
heave like a pummeled dough
with exiles revenant—
and eternity's throat
like a bell take note
'all all is well'—

look, it were better
in bitter meantime
to smile
and lift a glass—

the starts and stops,
brisk, becalmed,
distempered, sweet,
the sojourn short or long—

the outcome
in better hands
than ours.

★ ★ ★ ★ ★ ★ ★

Gerard
I cringe
in worst moments,
measure of mind
fails.
Horrid, a hand
blots out
the splendor,
the palette,
the covenantal arc.
All, all
goes black,
bleak,
into eclipse.

Until, until,
mercy walks beside,
a friend
half hidden
tenderly conniving
along Emrnaus way.

As if I
(the dispirited heart
cast away worthless,
as if
heartless were human—)
could so,
and not end

nowhere, an oblivion.

★ ★ ★ ★ ★ ★ ★

In accord with holy rule
'They shall dispose themselves
for God's glory, to be dispatched
here, there in the world'—

I ricochet
pillar to post
a fool decked out
in rags of time,
and hold
like a fuse lit, your words
counter to death—a dawn.

Thus we make do
Or I do.
(Imagination
a sound apothecary
healing first of all
fantastic, stuck, himself).

Good times and ill
I borrow voice
And chant your terrible
mantras, exorcisms
against the age's horrific eye,

by your leading,
by your sweetness
sir, by your grace—
bound whither?

always deeper and always
elsewhere.

* * * * * * *

In a rare lapse
from unencumbered soul
you saw Christ our Lord
in glory
tireless soldiering
blessing
our redcoats, our tars.

Come, construe
in high heaven
the meek One,
a far different
hue of hero

Mars, his toys
cast elsewhere
down, down
in a hellish heap

and that fair robe
reddened with His
and no enemy's

sanguinary stain

and those wounds
He tendered another
never once

but
cost beyond reckon
took to heart.

* * * * * * *

I wonder did you know
in your bones'
cave, vex, echo—

some day, astonishing day
(and you long absent from)
would confer grandly

rhyme, reason,
koan and its clue,
labyrinthe, light?

Let me in surrogate of
our 'least Society'
make much, give thanks for this

rich lode and legacy
we to this hour
(and who can tell
under what sun
of what millennium spent!)
draw mightily on.

Can it be, grief's grip
lets go, a century gone
when I

these words tardy,
nevertheless set down?
(eternity
cunningly crosshatching
time's blind free-hand)

a face
bent to you—'welcome
beloved, well done.'

* * * * * * *

I am so happy, so happy.
Thus were cruel matters gently cinched—
quietus of long drudgery.
                                        Of poetry, sweet prince
tardily crowned

and of pain
                                        steadily borne, a very
paragon.

What slows the breath amazed
and speeds the heart's arrow true,

what fruit and abundant attainment
long out of reach,
effortless

falls to,
quite fills,
spills over—

rejoice! is
yours

★ ★ ★ ★ ★ ★ ★

One day lacking death
a nemesis all in black
fed with massed papers
fires
where late
you sweetly breathed last.

What then was lost,
essence,
elixir of soul, taste, aftertaste—
never to know!
'Among firefolk, sitting in the air
count it all gain,' your counsel.
'Brooding, the Holy Ghost
has all by heart.'

(In a BBC broadcast in 1957, Lance Sieveking, a relative of G.M.H., told of an old man in Dublin who remembered passing the half-open door of Hopkins's rooms in St. Stephen's Green on the day after his death in 1889. Although it was June, a huge fire was burning in the grate, and when he turned to investigate, he saw 'an old fellow, all in black,' pulling out the contents of a chest of drawers and heaping papers on the fire.)

★ ★ ★ ★ ★ ★ ★

Gerard, I pray
(your crown of thorns
by Christ transfigured—
laurel, aureole, leaf of gold)

No base emulation
mar my love!

And then,
subtract
as you will,
this pittance too
from
heaven's vast store

22. Jubilee!

THE EVANGELIST

What meaning abides,
when the world's
machinations run amok,
the innocent
swept like debris aside,
irrationality enthroned?

The narrator
sober, clear eyed, labors
"that truth may emerge"

and lo
another generation
knows
perfidy and dishonor
naming, naming them
so
exorcising
their leaching power.

Knows also
nobility, high honor
self giving—
naming, naming,
sowing in time's furrow
hope against hope.

We know act and consequence,
Vainglory's rake's progress
victims torn asunder
the living gone under
victory's victim
bones dry bones.

And at center eye
that One
possessing his soul
under brute distress, duress

who dies then,
scorned, outlawed,
his tomb sealed
against lawless mischance,
the violation
we name resurrection.

It is faith violates
"*credo quia impossibile.*"
Faith rolls the stone aside,
timorous enters
the tomb,
resonant
as a Dead Sea cave
with the sworn word—
what could not be
and is.

SERMON ON THE MOUNT

Believers dismiss
(eminent intellects dismiss)
improbable commands

words come down, come down
the riven path of time
a babel of tongues
supersession of good.

"The jawbone of an ass
our exegete," cry
the ventriloquists of God.

"Love the enemy?
disproportionate burden!
see, malign wills
resisting unto death
the saving edge of truth
served up on Christian swords!"

The mountain falls like a wall—
alas, our lives.

Who now is fool
who wise?
the stones cry out
throats
of dumb stones

Abel, Christ
take the great thrust—
defection of the word—
the Christian sword.

THE PARALYTIC

Tempestuous calm
flat toned ranting
resigned resisting
they came—
this "court of last appeal"
"last ditch recourse"

The stories,
east west
immemorially alike;

all else failing,
hope vanished,
someone
stands on behalf—
(unguent touch breath
spittle clay
shadow)

Clumsily I speak
a zen paradigm
the all, the one
gathered in a napkin

The one the all!
envisioned
in those eyes

breathing bestowing
compassion

....

He entered a house—
crowds jostled overflowed
walls sagged groaned
Not an inch!

Pressing hard
room after room
brimming

Outside
curious, envious
rumors
like wild swallows
flying

Then
up the road
sidewise frontwise
like a crab—

strange entourage!
misery
wobbling hobbling
toward hope—

two men
bowed belaboring
a hammock a
backbreaking
portage—

"Our friend
no bones
no ifs
must be healed
this day!"

The gloomy chorus—
"You'll get no nearer
than the hundred feet
between
himself & you
where you stand.
Come
again
tomorrow!"

Torrents of advice
drones hangers on
helpful
as gravediggers.

But the two
(least of all
the afflicted one)
have not come so far
stood so near
to yield an inch
this hard won ground

Chatter
flows past his ear

the sick man
all eyes all desire
eyes the house
suppose suppose

No more ado
he signals
whispers close.

Then
before you can say,
"no hope" or
"give up" or
"come back tomorrow,"
the friend
handhold   foothold
clambers up top
dislodges the tiles!

The little house
rib cage to skin
breathes
like a whale   containing
someone named Jonah
someone named—

breathes hope!

The doom sayers—
a different tune
Bravo up there!

The inventive one
up top
crowing
like a cock
Come on
lend us a hand!

Infectious
they
climb up
like ancestors
seeking
progeny—

Hand him up now!

Inside—
no warning
heads swivel
astonishment
a bucolic
rehearsal of doomsday

Daylight for dark
the sky's falling in!

The helpless one
like a sorry clown
mickmocking
omnipotence
floats grandly down

recumbent pitiful
yes
misery yes
but—
a gleam in eye
that stolen fire
hope

Now Jesus,
a star turn?

PARABLE

Lilies of the field
speak volumes for me;
harvests laborious,
coins lost and found. Salt, light,

flowers pressed into
imagination's sweet devices;
the sea's abundant net drawn home,
good seed and ill, spent, forspent—

whatever hand or eye light on, my
pure delight draws forth
for healing balm of heart.
the arc above, unstained, starred with light

seven seas murmuring
teeming, bringing forth; am I not
their generative
imagination, interlocutor?

I draw semblances from thin air,
many, chaotic
thundrous hooves of wind—

one, sheaf and cluster
broken, pressed; the truth, the loaf
likened. Creation, hearkening
likening (glory!) you to me.

A DIALOGUE: THE GOOD SAMARITAN

"That story, that summons
from thin air drawn, left hanging there—
summed up; the best and worst of us."

"Like the three sided character
stepping smartly toward Jerusalem—
of three irresolute minds—
would flee, would pause, would stop."

"I picture him, three or one,
jolting along time's track.
A clock strikes, ear cocks;
dingdongbell, one, two, three.
Priest, levite, outsider.
        Time's flummery,
ordeal, dance; then

another bell, death knell—
near death in mid journey."

"Mere mockup humans, painted iron
tolling, telling, and all awry—
'All's well, God's world.'"

"We know it isn't—God's or well.
And what of the poor
wretch laid flat in the ditch?
Who's he? You, me?"

"Take it one further.
Those bandits
stripping the gospeler to his pelt
scuttling faceless off the page.
You, me?"

"Tell the time right!
It's not three of the clock
the somnolent hour, post prandial
post everything."

"Count the actors, a clue;
one traveler stripped bare, two
buzzing along, self important.
One pauses; importunate asks
What's going on here?
I count six hours, matin or compline hour.
Something ending or begun. But something."

"What make of one who makes
stories like that?"

"He's like a master clocksman, testing.
He's made time's figures—made time
Too—near nothing, mere something
the tracks, balances, wheels, bells had best
be obedient to."

"And we? Obedient or no?"

"Choice or mischance. He stands there
spinning the story; time's midtime,
time's end, no matter. Nothing's ended.
Those clock figures, trapped in time, let out
for merest show—"

"Christ plays in ten thousand places—
present tense, the big round number
laved in poetry; 'lovely in eyes
lovely in limbs not his.' "

"I dream sometimes, a sweet
revision and revenge
the robbers creeping back
shamefaced, giving over
rueful, their larceny."

"Mine is near nightmare, nightlong.
The scene; flat, edgy
a road named Chagrin. No terminus,
no origin. A smear of dust
dead as a snake's shed skin.
I muse on waking—the dream's about
trumpery eternity.
As though a snake of dust, its track
were all creation's story.
The snake vanishes, the road's a mere
base revision of our seven days.
Two walk that road, dazzled
with lofty pelagian fictions;
then, a slight discommoding.
As though the snake, trodden on, shuddered alive
throwing nice balance.
                    Someone lies there
hapless, human. Trouble.
                    A moment like a snake
invading, insulting the brain.
They pass by, hooded."

* * * * * * *

"You've not seen their faces?"

"I want to, I fear to.
Is it want or fear
mounts that anonymous quick evasion?"

PREMONITION

(Holy Thursday, Jesus speaks)

Delicious April   banquet in the offing
and shall I taste?
my soul   sorrowful
unto death.
Foreboding
a bird prating
one word only
death   mutters   metronomic   death
or   come   and again   come
into youth's
innate splendors
tentative showing.
My eyes drink
dawn's elixir
Young, young, my will
bends to time's rigors and rewards,
the long trek
into I know and know not—
Your writ is close; 'My promises prevail!'
the covenental arch stands firm
and I its fine-hewn keystone.
Banquet, I the bread thereof
fine as a mother's flesh, earth mother
Mary.
I, earth's vine and vat
inebriating ecstasy
So it is written;
'The word at word's end is—joy.
Let time like two lips conspire,

rehearse, have it by heart—joy!
But a shadow falls
befouling. Death.
Father let this cup pass—
or must all sweetness pass?
must death
a wrecking trespasser
scatter to four winds
the great board of creation?
O my Father
carrion makes mock
of sweet imaginings, their coming true
in You, in Me.
What shall be wrung
from this the world's vainglorious hour
sounding its tocsin
in my hands and side?

THE FRIDAY WE NAME GOOD

A penitent speaks

You come toward me
prestigious in your wounds,
those frail and speechless bones.

Your credentials:
dying somberly for others.
What a burden—
gratitude, fake and true vows,
crucifixes
grislier than the event—

and then the glory gap—
larger than life
begetting less than life,
pieties that strike healthy eyes
blind; believe! believe! Christians
tapping down the street
in harness to their seeing eye god.

Only in solitude
in passing tic of insight
gone as soon as granted—
I see you come toward me
free, free at last.

Can one befriend his God?
the question is inadmissible I know.
Nonetheless a fiery recognition
lights us;
broken by life
making our comeback.

SHALL THESE BONES LIVE

women
timorous
scarce daring
hope—
enter the tomb

impeding stone
like a papier-mâché
mockup
bounding downhill
in time
away, away—
death
passé

Within
majestic
white robed
someone
otherwise
unknown
save to wild surmise
seated
'at right hand.'

Of the women
we read
ecstasy
read terror
"ekstasos kai tremos"
held them in grip
They sought only
a corpse
—found
transfigured

a youth
alight
or an angel

"You seek Jesus
he is risen"

"ephugon" they fled
thenceforth
struck mute
"oudeni ouden"
uttered
not a word

Non resolution
consternation

Resurrection?

Of all endings
strangest
"ephobounto gar."
for
they feared greatly

Thus
from a harsh mask
our fate pronounced—

forbidden
the "good news?"

gar, because
the hinge upon which
we turn turn
this way
that
in time's
blind wind

Fear, silence
enforce
revaluation
of strange unwelcome
revelation

They said not a word

Yet
someone told

One to one
behind the hand
word sped
like
birds in midair
sipping ambrosia
winging away

Still
"he goes before you"
The broken circle
healed, closed

"I go before you"
toward we know
and know
not what

23. Isaiah

2:1 The word that Isaiah son of Amoz saw concerning Judah and Jerusalem.

2 Behold my mountain
touching high heaven,
the temple of God crowning all!
In that place,
the nations shall converge

3 crying:
"Come join with us
that Yahweh may teach us godly ways
as we walk in his paths!"

4 In that day, Arbiter over all,
God will judge the nations.
They will beat their swords into plowshares,
their spears into pruning knives.
Nevermore war
  never again!

5   "Come, let us walk
  in the light of Yahweh!"

9:2 The people who walked in darkness
  have seen a great light
at long last dawn.

3 You You You
joy harvest wealth

4 the yoke weighed heavy
the oppressors prodding
  hither yon
  us beasts of burden

5 boots
trod us under
blood reeking armor

Look!
all for naught
rot rust

6 a child wrought this
a son
His the power the glory
hagios athanatos
holy deathless One
iskyros strong One
emmanuel God with us

wisdom from on high
prince of peace
desired
of the everlasting hills

7 we pray
make firm
plant deep
justice, peace
now and forever

amen alleluia

11:1 From a barren stump
this tender shoot—
The One who is, is to come!

2 My servant, in him
spirit of counsel, of strong resolve,
of sure knowledge, of the fear of Yahweh.

3 For the little ones, the remnant
justice his passion.

4 His tongue lashes the violent
his breath a flame
consuming the wicked—

5 righteousness, fidelity
a cincture binding him close.

6 That day, My day
the wolf, the lamb
side by side,
the leopard, the goat—
calf and lion feeding together
and a little child
hither and yon
leading them

7 The cow, the bear—
their young side by side,
lions meek as lambs
feeding, imagine!
on the ox's straw

8 an infant
deep, fast asleep
in a viper's nest

9 No ravening wars, no evil
the land like a placid sea

tidal, susurrating,
permeated, animated
with knowledge of Yahweh!

22:1 Why this feverish
untimely rejoicing—
throngs on the housetops

2 parades snaking by,
flags, banners, slogans,
cannon volleys
all but extinguishing the sun?
Banqueting and revelry:

"Eat,drink!" they shout
"for tomorrow we die!"
I have news for you, sorry news.
Those "sons of the fatherland"
fell on no "field of honor,"

3 Your cause? tainted from the start.
How could it not end badly?

Death, death stalking the land!
death, arbiter, judge, usurper—

Hear me! Yahweh alone is God!
Malign revelers,
inconstant weathercocks!
this way, that, your hearts
reeling in mad winds!
ears itching, boots echoing
the throb of war drums—

4 Yahweh weeps.
Isaiah
keeps in his heart's vial,
the tears of God.

5 The holy city dissolves in darkness,
the warlike prevail!
the nation's heart grows vile—
panic, defeat, confusion.

Shout victory then
till the heavens shake
and the earth quakes—
you, the defeated victors!
. . . .

8 I name you anew.
No
you name yourselves—
Land of No Vision!

25:6 See, Yahweh prepares
on this holy mountain
a surpassing feast!
Only imagine—
for one and all
fat of the marrow,
ambrosial wines!

7 Here, on this mountain
God sweeps aside
the veil of sorrow,
the cloth of mourning—

8 death no more!
balm in Gilead!
heal-all upon every wound!

O day, we entreat, come soonl

42:1 Comes now my servant;
look how I upbear her,
this chosen one
in whom my soul delights!
My spirit outpoured,
my justice her own!

2 Her mind no proving ground
whence vexing thoughts bestir,
how gently she walks the earth!
small creatures safe and sound,
unharmed, close cherished.

3 Her soul
borne on high
an unextinguished flame
routing the dark.

4 Faithful, unconquerable—
the ends of the earth hearken,
lauding that Word of truth—
her, my own!

42:5 In the beginning
(I the beginning)
all things left my hand.
You, clay gently kneaded.
Lover, mouth to mouth,
I breathed,
you breathed, newborn.

6 Now hand in hand
we walk the world.
You, as though clean parchment—
my covenant, your flesh
writ. You, the living text.

7 My work, my wonders, yours;
to open blind eyes
to lead forth the captives!
. . . .
8 These, yes
ever greater works, await!

My servant!
a victim
borne to the abattoir,
a plant languishing
in sterile ground

in guise scarcely human,
no dignity, no beauty—
despised, rejected,
beneath notice utterly.

Snatched from among the living
condemned by sinners—
who worked this infamy?

Dissembling, desperate,
clamorous with;
            Ave Caesar!
It was for us, the lost,
for us she suffered.

But see—
an Easter dawn,

a flood of light!
the world to come
at long last, come!

24. Plowshares Poems

SWORDS INTO PLOWSHARES

Everything enhances, everything
gives glory—everything!

Between bark and bite
Judge Salus's undermined soul
betrays him, mutters
very alleluias.

The iron cells—
row on row of rose trellised
mansions, bridal chambers!

Curses, vans, keys, guards—behold
the imperial lions of our vast acres!

And when hammers come down
and our years are tossed to four winds—

why, flowers blind the eye, the saints
pelt us with flowers!

For every hour
scant with discomfort
(the mastiff's baleful eye,
the bailiff's mastery)—

see, the Lord's hands heap
eon upon eon,
like fruit bowls at a feast.

THOSE I LOVE

Those I love
are trundled off to jail.
Fear gnaws me,
madmen toss

the explosive law
into our gentle midst,
our joined hands—
children from parent,
spouse from lover, violently torn.

By night only night,
night by day.
The cross we cling to
kills us

I hear tortured Christ;
'Not all, no, not all!
turn, page;
stone,
roll back.'

LATTER DAY PRISON POEMS

1) My Brother's Battered Bible, Carried into Prison Repeatedly

That book
livid with thumb prints,
  underscorings, lashes—
I see you carry it
into the cave of storms, past the storms.
I see you underscore
like the score of music
all that travail
that furious unexplained joy.

A book! the guards
shake it out for contraband—
the apostles wail, the women
breathe deep as Cumaean sibyls,
Herod screams like a souped up record.

They toss it back, harmless.
Now, seated on a cell bunk

you play the pages slowly, slowly
a lifeline humming with the song
of the jeweled fish, all but taken.

2) Prisoners in Transit

They took the prisoners, willy-nilly
on death's own outing
shod like dray horses
jump suits   pied like mardi gras
& curses & groans & ten pound shoes
& starts & stops
at every
station of the cross
across Wm Penn's
Sylvania

'Here's where that first trouble-
shooter started his last mile,' the guard yelled
   through his bull horn mouth—

'& here he did a phony fall—
gaining time was all
'& here it was
he rained like a red cloud
& here
we built his everloving ass
an everlasting memorial—

'this mile square Christian tomb
& closed the book

'You may all
come down now
take a 3 to 10 year
close look.'

3) Poverty

A prisoner is very poor—
1 face, 2 arms, 2 hands, 1 nose, 1 mouth

also 3 walls
1 ceiling
10 or 12 iron bars—
then if lucky
1 tree
making it, making it
in hell's dry season

I almost forgot—
no legs!
contraband! seized!
they stand stock still
in the warden's closet.
There like buried eyes
they await the world.

4) Zip Code

The precious info—
your whereabouts in the maze—
'Camphill Prison, Pa.' I memorize it
down to the absurd
talisman 1 7 O 1 1

Open Sesame!
the tomb shudders
a crack opens,
this wafer of life
slips through.

5.) A Few Gifts for the Prisoner

The sea, a bearded mime
mimicking lambs and lions

The sun
betokening variety and
crystalline steadfastness.

Then one or two gestures of children
seizing, tossing, meandering—

like the prisoners, making
much of little.

Then an episode
of Luke's gospel; healing.
Let the prisoner bear that gift
onward, hands incorrupt, empty.

In and out of his cell
a flea circus trooping
too small for the guards' gimlet.

Let Christmas come around
for the prisoner alone—
cold, deprived, true.

And the angel
who succorded Peter in chains—
enters
the prisoner's soul, whispers
Magisterially; Not yet, No
Not yet.

6) Time

To gain time
you must waste time
the 'waste'
an undercurrent—
passion, plethora

The smile, the daredevil eyes
More of same!
they bespeak
opposites, ironies,
repose, tears.

Gaining time, wasting time—
who shall do both?

a unitive fricative act
strikes sparks, blazes up,
reproves dire necessity,
burns away
irresponsibility.

Short of death's caught breath

I think of 'doing time.'
O my brother
when Christ steps
into time's
uncontrollable current
like a swimmer answering a cry—
He must do time—
those arms like wheels, that beat,
that nearing mercy

You
near. And He
mercy's sense and savior
grows, near.

7) Penalties

You in prison
I so to speak, at large
taste the penalty too—
half a world
half a loaf

like a two-legged dog
I saw once
body precariously balanced—
left front leg
right hind leg

tottering about, image
of half a soul

so to speak, alive
in the so called world—

the hunger, the
half a loaf called life

8) Your Second Sight

Walking by the sea
I put on
like glasses
on a squinting
shortsighted soul—

your second sight

and I see
washed ashore
the last hour of the world—

the murdered clock of Hiroshima.

TO ELIZABETH IN PRISON

Like a north star and its child
you shine there
among the wandering and lost
the stupefied, the victimized.

O my dear, there is gravity
and there is grace, and you
like a Vermeer woman
holding aloft a scales,
her face flooded with light
(the window open to pure day)—
must weigh, be not
found wanting.

TO THE PLOWSHARES PRISONERS, WITH LOVE

Dear ones
You'll be dumfounded to hear it;
through your stern confining
I'm the beneficiary
of a literacy campaign.

The abc's of soul
I crawl over
like a botanist a
moon pit
a surgeon over a brain

Now I write and read
and publish abroad
the lost sense of the tribe—

in moon dust a sign
no dead moons!

a scrawl
a footfall
a befalling

ROOT

"To love selflessly . . . with a strength equal to the square root of distance, is the task of our hearts while we are children."

—Boris Pasternak

The square root of realilty
escapes us quite.
Whereas
the round root, the tortured root, the root
sharp pointed as an arrowhead—

this I celebrate and fear, and despite fear
keep digging toward, for all the world as though
life depended, or death, or a feverish cry

wrung from the throat of stocks and stones.

No death until
I hold the talisman
and taste—
                some say 'beware poison.'
                    Some
wiser, dare
                    'Until, you will not live.'

PAX CHRISTI–SPIRIT OF LIFE PLOWSHARES

(North Carolina, 1994)

1. The Court

Someone commands;
(the voice of the heart)
'Poetry, even here!'

Obstacles; a brisk frisking,
descent among the dead,
worms fleeing into wormwood.
Portraits, faces
giving faces away, by Bosch.

Then the judge. A phiz like tallow's
sickly light,
night closing in. A Dogsberry,
don't tell him, he's
on leash, on loan to mercy.
'Time, twice time, half a time'—
dead fingers
conjugate apocalypse.

A gargoyle cries; All rise!
High, mighty, a soul in torment
turns to slime.

2. Judge

An epiphany—impeccable, impervious.
Is. From the beginning.
A triphammer for heart,
a piledriver look
laid the foundations.
Before him, nothing.

Foursquare, for judgment,
he laid out the world
you fondly thought was Christ's,
some gospel said so. No.

Seek no further
He's the great Why
guns are red eyed,
cops round bellied, the FBI
ax jawed, oak. Why
pay checks snow like manna
minions tread softly
juries quiver like catgut
under the punishing
suave bow of the maestro.

A baleful look,
and you'd better
hastily put on masks, sheep or goats,
baaing to right, butting to left.

And the walleyed totems
outstare you, big as billboards
wall to wall.
Primordial, stony, they turn
mere mortals to stone—

Always always
origins, the ace of starts—
judge begets judge,
judge clones judge
judge issues
from forehead of judge,
& naked, demure, subsuming
Venus hermaphrodite,
judge hoists his hosanna
steers a half shell ashore—

O you could talk
autonomy, dignity
till the gavel struck winter
and the words winged south—
but he holds court
tight as a lockup
tighter than lockdown

and the sheep
baptised in the blood
of a stillborn lamb,
and pneumatic as blimps
beatific ascend

and presto! the guillotine
speedy as centipedes
snicks & snees
goats to their knees.

3. The Verdict

The first day, my brother stood.
Sun shed dark
and leonine stood beside.

The second, I followed, somewhat.
The third to week's end
I leave to you to know.

Leave it to him,
his dignity, care, cue and—crime.
Something seen, said, done. Lips moving
as though under water;
words himalayan,
air thin, hardy
birds faint and fall.

Let's sit here and wait—
all we may, for the end.
Obey the prophets who say; wait
the benchwarmers, beggars.

Look; against all evidence, sun
shakes the dark once again.
Stands
to say so.

4. The Opposite

Writing. I think; here's my hand
grown older, no matter. Weaving this web
like any spider, called words.
Here, there ranging, hello brother.
No matter who—my brother.

What's the opposite hard consonant
to web, web, airy weaving?
What's the wholly opposite, what's
all teeth, edgy, fricative,
so frontal and free
it breaks the metal cuffs of sheriffs,
gives wrists their hands, hands their
paintings, pianos, poems—

hand to hand, the children,
the dance of time yes, and
no need of no, after years of no?

5. The Prisoner, the Cave

Ancients are writing with pencil stubs
scriptures in a cave.
What will be, what was
is, is, is in the cave.

Patience, a crystal, tells the time;
that and a cry, How long O Lord. That
and no reply. None,
and the outcry!

The parchment unrolls as they write—
a sky, a beyond,
a flying carpet, a throne
whence issue thunders; Thus Sayeth.

Love one another, they write. They love.

The cave is a pock on the moon.
The moon wastes and wanders,
a sea guarding its salt.

Unrolled one day, the scroll
will stutter, whisper, keen, thunder—
too low a pitch for humans,
lions plotting
the last day of the lamb;
a pitch too high, angels
rehearsing apocalypse.

6. The Gift

It's measureless
Only the image, Son
of the ineffable, takes its measure.

Like this;
joined hands, hardly seen
(dusk to dark on the instant)

behind bars, beyond all barring
a beseeching; have mercy
on the merciless!

Like this, the measure;
he casts ahead like a fly fisherman—
Torment, truth. The take.

7. I Want You Free

Intemperate, temperate be damned.
I want tempers riled, want
vile matters resolved.
I want you free.

(No urge
to wax metaphysical, metaphorical
like puppeteers in pulpits—
'Of course you're free!')

Justice?
The word's a smear or sneer,
the locks guttural as guards.
No key turns, no tongued
freedom bell intoning 'free!'
Nothing. Bars adamant
as justice held, withheld.

Nothing?
No.
My love, the poem.

25. Diary of Sorts

DIARY OF SORTS

Fifty years on earth—
I, in prison.

Now at sixty
prison, my lot.

Thus I translate;
'putting away the things of a child.'

EIGHT DAYS IN SWEDEN

(1974; the tiger cages, Vietnam)

Imagine; I'm the prisoners' public voice,I crawl like a bug up
& down the world's blank phiz,

shouting in stone ears. Yesterday in the Swede boondocks
marxists chomped their potatoes, watching with boiled eyes

me, sweating my soul for the lost tribes, the bones rotting in
Saigon cages.

Absurd theatre my meat, a dash of cruelty. I tell my soul;
don't turn intellectual mugger,
don't sweat despairing bullets in hotel rooms.

Believe, believe.

Believe? You're a lifelong slave, a dwarf
shouldering the scenery of some dark demonic scene;
you're

a brush in a pot of pig's blood, scrawling the title of a one
night stand named
'Candle In The Cave'; Or, 'The Bats Revealed As Right After All
Though Blind As Humans And Upside Down.'

Sweet distant brothers, sisters, save my soul.

ON ATTAINING FIFTY-THREE YEARS IN NEW YORK, ALLELUIA!

1.

Air comes
up an alley, down a flue
like inhaling a charred mattress

Who sees straight?
who knows where?

Religion? the mediators
shuffle on turkey feet, side-
stepping the ax

Anyone hearing them
would rush off
to Yonkers New York
gun capital of the world
and sell his soul
for a snub nose Nick Carter six!

2.

My generation was stillborn
I saw them in prison—
the con men with priest faces
airbrushed skin
souls ground to salt

No savor.
Irish crooks, Irish priests
I saw them melt
in their own juices
mewing in sleep
Vietnam Vietnam

3.

Not a clue.
Retarded as fence posts
guarding the flocks & herds of empire—
the winds went by
the wars went by

we were born to the bucks
we were worlds apart

When we burned away
they kicked the ash
turned up
face up
our bad luck;
no heart.

THE DIGGERS
(of graves on the White House lawn)

having no future
which is to say
renouncing
all hardsell
trumpery and tricks

we strike free
for the work ordained—
digging in, in, in,
uncovering the dead
present, buried alive.

HERE WE GO AGAIN (1)
(Pentagon, 1978)

Jerry hustles his frame
off to D.C.

Yet another arrest
at the boiling cauldron.

Phil, jailed for the duration
a stone in a well bottom.

Where is the ark, I cry?
where my land?
soul hovers between—

My bird brain
alights on a green tree.
I'll pluck the sprig of life, bear it
back to the indicted, stalled
wondrous lovers of life.

HERE WE GO AGAIN (2)

I come in
a floating buddha
for whom
prosperity, adversity
are buzzing flies
on flowerlike eyelids.
I stretch my arms
draw them into
amber
time

ODE TO THE SHROUD OF TURIN

(Berkeley, '79)

High in the theological hills
beyond Mount Huff & Puff
Mount Scrutiny & Squint

they 'carbon test' the Shroud of Turin.

The mind's sorry ebb.
An inconclusive Christ
all shadow
may have reposed there, dead to the world—
'asphyxiation, following on
prolonged suspension
on a vertical gibbet.'

May have reposed there, may not.

I see
the homeless huddled in doorways,
the unentailed rich
grabbing their swag, running off the page.

Then the doomed One, the Stranger
muttering blessings
no one buys

He walks abroad in the day
half clothed
like a mad mullah,
his painted rag
glorious, sumptuous,
a peacock
eyed
with his own eye.

PRISONERS; THE IRISH FAST AND DIE

(Long Kesh, Belfast, 1980)

Burden of the evening; Long Kesh.

A fifty mile highway,
a moonlit swath,
the young Irishman

voluble and mournful
his mood
inconsequential
to the plight of dying prisoners.

(His gloom, its incitement—pure American—
gnawing unhappiness, slavish job)

The eerily perfect dark,
a full moon suspended,
he whining, keening away

we voyagers
enclosed in a silver capsule
shot perfectly
toward an imperfect future—
moody, feverish, thwarted
even as granted.

And across wild waters
young men lay sleepless,
papery skulls, sunken eyes
swathed like the unborn
in a caul of vision.

ANOTHER BIRTHDAY, IMAGINE!

The shadow
is 64 years long.
Ungainly it shambles, muttering to itself
(a shadow, a showdown)
Grow old! Grow old!

Dawn is up.
With the man walks
        a smear of shadow.
He sings to himself
disowning;

Darkness
cast by me, begone from me.

His soul
he holds like a burning glass before.
A concentrate of dawn
burns in him—
soul, his own.

PIE IN THE SKY

As governor of Arkansas and a candidate for president, Clinton flew home to witness the execution of lobotomized Ricky Rector. Led from his cell to the electric chair, the prisoner left the pie from his last meal in his cell, intending to eat it after his execution.

Someday somehow Ill get me
makeup of that pie
Rick shoved forkfuls of
into his soon to be
resurrected tummy
treadin, yumyumin among the
dead men walking
& hummin no doubt, and strummin
'America the beautiful.'

Why just imagine, the same
current that baked the All-
American confection
sent Rick shooting praises
altitudinous, the pie
like unto him combusted
like unto him alas
eternally
unconsumed.
Who I ask my soul
the savvy baker of this

(turned executioner—
but don't
dwell on this or that—
apples, lard, flour,
rolled out flat—
blood, bone, pore addled brain,
recipe close kept
as a sheriff's keys—
   who lo, hath wrought this wonder?

      Why pore Rick doesnt know
      his ars from a baked apple.
      Then drag him outa there for
      fifty quickened paces,
      a made-up word sufficing
urging 'Cmon Rick, quick like—
   ex-e-cu-tion, ex-ha-la-tion,
      ex-cavation'—
      then KABOOM!
      what he dont know wont hurt him.

      Sure kid cross my heart we'll
bring you right back here yer
      just desserts awaiting.

CHICAGO

(Holy Week, 1994)

A thought; we were done with winter.
   but the Great Lake leapt,
            a warrior at our throat.
         We were stuck like tires in muck.
      Back to back, cold shoulder
        December jostling April
         ungodly, a grimace.

A thought; we were done with death
a respite, after the run of it,
the planet tilted crazy, winds
winded utterly.

The long run of the drama drains the heart—
wreckage of genesis
The Calvary rout. The trio. Bad cursing good.
And at center pole, run through,
the One we long to be done with, desperate
(no second chances, death in the offing?)
if we could! If only He would
like the one to right or left of His hand
die and be done with.

CARDINAL

I mull about
in the grab bag of the mind
(fits, starts, vague scraps,
intentions raveled, faded)—
then
forgiveness.
Let us forgive one another.
Better, let us pray;
O cloud
of murdered witnesses, forgive
our furtive or bold trespass
on sacred ground,
our hatreds diffused, denied
in soulless sacred jargon.

Cardinal, let us kneel,
ask pardon of murdered children
of Vietnam, of Salvador.

The children bathe us
with cupped hands, our tears
lo! innocent as theirs.

I APPEAR ON A TELEVISION IN DENVER, COLORADO, A DOWNER

Reader, why read on?

because this mortal body shall
put on immortality?
or because
incongruity lurks,
motley in bells, a fool?

—comes to mind
a fountain, a public square
a Belgian town.
A little bronze boy
pissing
in a stone basin.

Summer autumn winter
no defector he, let years
take their toll, elsewhere.
Like Huck Finn
he poles time's
lazy current, makes mock—
those who merely boringly
grow up, fade fast.

The sun fuels his heart, moons
meander by, a cold caress.
Stars in orbit crown the task. Behold
an ikon of sweetness;
his little handy dandy
harmlessly

jets forth, pure, pearly,
prelapsarian, a fountain in the first
garden of all!

In the basin
trout
sputter and thrive and

strollers take delight.

Schoolboys of an age,
wicked, emulous
clot together, gleeful
draw from schoolboy pants,
theirs too—
the mocking malfeasant
conspiratorial tools wagging.

Staid matrons, moms, nurses
run and run toward—
bearing on high
like pennants, small underpants—
coo, child! come cover yourself!

To no avail.
Our boy's like the three
who sing 'praise ye'
this child
of raging metals, tried by fire.

He holds in hand
the 'logos spermaticum'
I think he
created the world
the child maker of all

Little boy relieve us
believe for us—
all things
are good.

MIMI

We kept watch with Mimi dying.
Miles away, soul
kept tugging back.
You've seen
a daredevil falling,
   then landing safe,
  ease, ease the parachute home.

That's not soul. Soul is wind
against silk, racing counter.
Nor a kite—soul's not a kite,
soul is wind; that
animate thing, dipping, prancing,
is merest clue.

The holy bread touched lip
pale as shot silk. We kept watch, intoning
'Body of Christ.' Then; wind,
a bird, a bird like wind
quicker than ravens in parables of wind—

What goes counter? where?
(we cried) and why
always elsewhere?

We saw nothing, and we knew.

APARTMENT 11-L

1.

I dwell in rooms
that came together from four winds
help of a flying carpet,
Aladdin's lamp,
and 200 friends at the least.
Rooms of faces and words.

The typewriter spouts, happy as coffee fresh.
Chairs, rickety and serviceable
hold out their arms.
Ingredients, beans, barley, butter, rice
implore from shelves and cupboards—
O make of us something frivolous, original
and your soul will abide content
and sprout blossoms and apples
like a tree in a body named Eden!
Busybody pots and pans
clatter like Dutch housewives—
Fill us with music, ambrosia, nectar!
Roots at window; Let me tell
how these green children fail or multiply
panting like dogs in noon, for water
water on the tongue.

And here, I almost forgot.
the door to a dark
underground drama.
Faces walk off the walls
into my theatre of dreams, good dreams.
At dawn
the faces depart, like
mimes of the Bread and Puppet troupe,
where they made foolish sense all night
of rational mad days.
So I can say
truthfully; Now I see
and kiss my hand to those I love
who put on once more
on a wall of no wailing
their set expression, ikons and ancestors;
Thank you, now I see.

2.

These are the rooms I go from.
An angel commands it; Go from here.

I go
to break the bones of death, to crack
the code of havocking dreams. I go from here
to judgment, to judges
by Rouault, Daumier, Goya,
their hammer crack of doom.
I go. Then, I'm told
by a guardian angel of the rooms I'm told—
When you go from here
faces of those you love
turn to the wall, and weep.
I have an angel's word.

And when I return
older, sad at times, so little of death undone
despite all sacrifice and rage
Lo, something savory, exotic
steams in a pot, the table fitly laid.

And the typewriter's iron mask
melts in a smile, and the keys
like a lover's hands
compose a love letter;
Welcome. Believe. Endure.

RIVER

(to my mother)

Moving
like a woman
drowned
toward
nothing
but the sea—

'No
not dead!

the sun
falls to my breast
a torch.
Look
I burn
bridges
behind me.'

ON BEING A CERTAIN KIND OF JESUIT

Watch
the one who watches—
he sees
(is)
neither winner
nor loser

those eyes—
maybe
a kind of pivot
of it all

INSIGHT

When I look, I see
I've spent my life seeing—
under that flat stone, what?
why that star off kilter?

Turn Turn! I intoned, and
out of the stone there stood
What-Not in a white garment.

Jacob's ladder descended
(the angels holding steady)—

I mounted and I
saw
what

I SWEAR IT

Isn't for me.
An old country dog
I hang out on God Almighty's back porch
snoozing. Leaving the world's outcome
to the hand I see sometimes
covered with grave spots,
stroking my pelt.

They say He tends the engine,
hit or miss,
stop and go.
                    Take it, say I, it's all
yours,
              everything but
the warm grained boards under me
and three steps down
                         to beyond.

LETTER

Dear friends
I live
in haunts
in hatches
in sacristies
in solstices
in clefts of trees

ashamed as clocks awry
in universities that cry
I AM THE UNIVERSE

Dear Friends
in the failed church
in the flamboyant state
in the cycling heart of youth
that concocts
of rock & punk
needles & chills
a music   a drug

misnamed 'here'
misbegotten 'now'

GETTING OLD

I saw priests
like wintry wigs
or raveled birds' nests—

In despair, in youth
I longed for the day
I'd simmer down
old wine in an old bag
insipid, tractable
a necrophiliac
toward the tunnel's end.

Your gut was god
you were exemplary in the crotch
(which in marxist morphology
withered away
in the blossoming kingdom
—hyacinth, wisteria—
no Eve at the trellis rising
no moon, madness, mouth)

All a lie!
the fiery grow old fiery,
naked as a whipstock.

The sun huffs like an adder
burn baby burn
everything burns
sanity, eyeballs;
middle age is cursing God

antistrophe
to that sublime dawn bird
that sang its preincarnate
maidenhood, murder.

Now I remember.

And
if I dance
algebraic as an angel
it is
because You are
intricate motive
staggering burden—
old Father I heft and shoulder
out of the burning city.

COURAGE AND THEN SOME

They call me courageous; they take
their measure, not mine;
                                                  mine
a face in a crowd, a voice among voices.

If I say no, I learned the numb syllable
from withstanding ancestors
holding the witless infant upright.
From gravity to grace I came
untaught, all beholden.
Walking toward, my measure is
a golden house
where suns shelter at sundown.

Sleeping, my measure is
illimitable death, not proud.

LESS THAN

The trouble was not excellence.
I carried that secret,
a laugh up my sleeve
all the public years
all the lonely years
(one and the same)
years that battered like a wind tunnel
years
like a yawn at an auction
(all the same)

Courage was not the fault
years they carried me shoulder high
years they ate me like a sandwich
(one and the same)

the fault was—dearth of courage
the bread only so-so
the beer near beer

I kept the secret under my shirt
like a fox's lively tooth, called
self knowledge.

That way
the fox eats me
before I rot.

That way I keep measure—
neither Pascal's emanation
naked, appalled
'under the infinite starry spaces'
nor a stumblebum

havocking
in Alice's doll house.

Never the less!
Summon
courage, excellence!

The two, I reflect, could
snatch us from ruin.

A fairly modest urging—
Don't kill, whatever pretext.
Leave the world unbefouled.
Don't hoard.
Stand somewhere.

And up to this hour
(Don't tell a soul)
here I am.

26. Beyond

BEYOND

What lies beyond—-
Beyond scope and skill,
beyond
wayward winds, capricious minds,
beyond, beyond despair—

lies within, plenary and pure—
compassion's clear eyed child.

What lies beyond,
beyond
dole and bribe and
browbeating eyes,
beyond mandated terror—
lies, within;
                    I mean
solace, end time
sweetly present
in sad or gladsome hours—
creator Spirit, hand in mine,
a ringaround, pure light.

What lies beyond,
(diaphanous, denied,
beyond
          the death of promise)—
lies within.

Hear it;
the golden tongued
choral ode of the unborn.

LIVING

Thirty years;
on Carpenter Hill the story ends.

At most, fifty years—
Merton's span, when the span tore free.

By whose will or whim
do I flog along, a nag
at odds with the world?—
Two left feet, or
a foot in his mouth
as the Irish say.

I wish and wish;
O could I map the way!
could the road, like a wayward runner
change its mind!
could I toss the rider
who galls my guts!

three wishes?
You'll rue their granting, the Irish say.
Listen. The map is a map of mind
it burns like a branding iron.
The road will rise, will
coil your throat like a noose.
The rider weighs three hundred stone—
claim and clamor
and Christopher's terrible child.

ONCE FOR ALL

Overvaulting death's
vaunt and taunt—
my love for you,
which like dawn to full day
or a child unborn
is coming, true.

I PRAY

clarity
one day

on this
(called
and miscalled)—
life.
Clarity, and
no broken sunrise
no promise broken
that promised fair play
and shortly, no
betrayed, fell in pieces—
impersonal, grand, and no recourse.

As though
(miscalled) life
decreed;
mine to confer,
yours to make do.

SAVIORS

I see the tired bemoaning look of saviors,
the market *Salvation* bottomed out.
I see time unredeemed, stowed away
like honey gone sour in dead trees
that green once, firm grounded our destiny.

What so redundant as a seventy-year old
savior, stuck among statuary?

O cunning Christ, unhanding, handing on
your bloody destiny!
                                        I peer into faces
unseen these thirty years.

What do I seek? what do they seek of me?
Outcry? an aggravating gospel?

                                                        Unlucky we,
our boats becalmed, unseaworthy
that once rode like chargers the mauling sea.

Clichés like lips of tidal waters
touch, sigh, dissolve the keen tyro's look
that took for prey once
world and its waters, with fond arrogance.

KNOWLEDGE

Everything known beforehand
except
the hand from a cloud
releasing the rain's largesse,
binding rain like sheaves.

Except
the hand from the ark
freeing a dove in air

except
the dove
blind, affrighted, tossed
on the watery void

except You
lodged there, living, secret,
the world's nest egg

from whose birth
rises our only
hand   ark   dove

THE WOUND

I have endured more
in the plight of those I love
than ever in my flesh.

The plight is consequence.
The cause is steadfastness.

I tremble for their fate.
The rub is raw.
Relief?

We die, the mortal
wound is one, another.

THE BIRD

An ancient monk wrote:
'The years of our life—like a storm driven bird
blown through the rafters of a great hall
alight, warm, loud with celebration—
through the gauntlet of air, it flutters and runs frantic—
then shortly up and out again, vanishing in night.'

Another image.
In the cliffside cottage one summer day
a witless bird struck full force the window glass,
fell, to all evidence dead,
smoke from a snuffed match.

I took the feathery morsel in hand, cozened, stroked,
then held the dummkopf
under a water spout.

With a puny flutter, it came to.
Out of doors, I tossed it in air. It ran
like a chastened kid—
rum dumb as a thumped drum.

Well, raise a jar
to dim wits and second chances.

THE SEA

is known
only to the poem—
a sorry and secret thing
like the grief of a lorn mother

I know this:
the times
a voracious sea
destroy
the sons of mothers.

The poem lived once
by 'is', by 'has'—
now
from the sea's throat
a roar—
'Must!'

To herself
the mother thinks:
I am the measure.
My grief. Welcome death.

The poem seizes her,
the sea shakes its mane; 'No!'

The sea's implacable reach,
the bed that east to west
makes a myth of the son

makes her too; must.
Takes her measure; more.

DOMESTIC WEATHER REPORT

No great miracles for us
Not even small ones,
nothing of the sort.

(They're terra incognita, lunar.)
Omega doesn't walk there, even anonymous.)

From my brothers, my friends
I come on a dark clue—
eyes that see,
ears taking note,
the heart heard from,
the tongue, a prisoner of conscience
learning truthful words, and
expedient, silence.

Thus (eventual!) the human, difficult, step by step, hard won
glory.

SEEKING

What I didn't seek, came.
High voltage. Danger. The famous & rich.

Then in great numbers and days, the lucky—
untouched by the leprous hand, Success
that fits shrouds with pockets,
turns Croesus, evasive and average
head to sole, to deaf and dumb gold.

What I sought didn't arrive at first.
I sat for hours, years, in the buddha's palm

or paced here to horizon
like a psalmist
halfway through a dirge
or a halfhearted alleluia
(God the reluctant prompter)

the train I ticketed
irretrievable, over the hill, no angel
to speak of

Until.

WORD

I'm seeking a word.
Unknown, and I unable.
Imagine, 74, seeking a word.
Like an infant, the first word of the tongue.
From milk, murk and memory
how do I make a word,
which must at all cost, be the first?
a word beyond foretelling
like eyes unborn,

whose color
unknown, unable
will paint the colors of the world.

TELL ME

I wonder why
if life is 'goodness and truth'
poems don't spring at fingers' ends,
why this 'labor limae,'
why Michelangelo et al
belabor stones for entrance
into resurrection, no simple
accord with gravity or grace, rolling back.
Why ends don't meet, like friends

after long aching absence.
Why the poor die poor
and the rich hardly ever.

I pray; Tell me
but You don't
Who told our Father
daily bread is due, and
let go debts—
Why this world? when a better

Some anonymous man of the road could

on a bitter night
with two cold hands
and small skill
knock together.

TAKE YOUR CHOICE

I think to myself
I believe in God. Nothing. And if I think

I believe in no God, nothing.

Does the sun believe in God? If the sun
disbelieves, is it banished?
Or the wind exiled, if it shouts Nay?

It is the absence, the dead mouth
no beat of a heart, the world
grown irregardless, witless—

white stones on a dark path
and at wit's and will's end, the darker stark house.

CONFESSION

You should see my heart
the way I do. But no, never

the way I do.

It looks like this;
a look of spiders
half seen, seeing,
spiders weaving
scriptures in a cave.

You've got to be blind
to bluff like this;
heart beats so steady
you'd say to hear it;
there goes rough and ready!
How wrong you'd be!

Think of a prisoner
at midnight, when memory
turns, tosses the heart
like meat on a spit

Or the look of a prisoner
brought out a dawn
dead on the books;
hung with a crude sign;
conscience, consequence.

Wearied, heart scrawls
a shingle that reads;
'Gone. Dawn fishing.'

Be sure, be sorry;
alas, No catch.
Salmon dawn slips through.

GOD SPEAKS
(for a 73rd birthday)

I could gather him in
with a limber swing of the scythe.
The reaper is ready, eyes alert.
But to what avail?

All ways to the throne he'd dig heels in,
the unborn poems
raving like banshees, horrific.

He'd plead and plead—
justice unraveled, the City
half built, half in ruins, and who takes note?
He'd summon a witnessing cloud,
the ragtag of his streets—
'Let be, let him be; who more will have mercy,
a coin in the palm, a word mitigating?'

Shameless, a skilled ranter,
He'd hail my Son to court.
'Tell all, the fortunes and follies.
Fidelities, tell.
And did you not, crisis impending,
and moved to tears at his plight
dispatch a myriad of guardian spirits?'

Reluctantly therefore, the verdict.

Sentence commuted for as long
as the poems lament, unborn.
As long as the poor draw breath, and abate.
As long
as the river of life is befouled
and the City's lamp unlit.
As long as swords are drawn and plowshares rust.
As long as the bombers prowl.

As long as at large
the lion ravens the lamb.

THE ECONOMY IS BULLISH

I hear how Mammon prospers
from the woman on the street
who has nothing but the street.

Each night she rolls up the pavement
like a goose-down blanket.
All weathers, she's cozy there.

Each day
in the brows of power brokers,
she wheels and deals
humming along
with the whirring Stock Exchange.

She wears triage like a billboard,
tricked out in ticker tape
laying bets like Mother Courage—
A hundred to one, a square meal, she moans
Cmon baby give!

Then
off she pushes in harness.
She's tomorrow
Pushing today away.

She's the next war.

CHARIOT

We're sane as the dawn
that consents, creates
time and again, our world.

Let's help, let's flog.
the flanks of the chargers
that lift the sun aloft
against all odds—
horses, horseman Apollo
so beautiful
so overrated.

I'd rather be at mercy
of someone less appalling
less breakneck.
Someone—steadfast
even stuck.

I'd say we're stuck.
I'd say—that's a start.

Maybe—go from there?
Maybe
Someone's at our side who
(get up, up!)
died under the wheels.

EGO LIGHTLY

In my face—
a toad with a plowed brow
and a 3 sided leer
uninherited
as the stitched mouth of a corpse—
in sum, a face
you wouldn't kiss for mother's.

Visible
                to me only
(I won't tell)
in the knobby brow—
a jewel like a third eye.

It blinks in code
to me, like this;
You're a prince you know—
don't you
and I
won't tell.

MY COUNTRY 'TIS OF THEE

        So difficult a love
made bearable
by you and your

face near mine
after all
smog, spittle, rhetoric,
vaunting smug valor, war upon war
like toad humping toad,
sweaty, bugeyed to make
what can't be—
the fairy tale at term,
a princeling people
emerging entire
to huzzahs, merry midwives, the world
a rocking rollicking cradle.

Not like that.
Let's you and I
bypass the foolishment, get born.
Prince, pauper, what matter?
let's proffer
true, tomorrow.

COTTAGE INDUSTRY

I thought to sing aloud
a simple poem
quaker or shaker—
the world a waxed floor
showing us back
heel to head, a
theology, anthropology
simple, turn turn turn

No. Such complexities, what a fond fool!

We spin like spiders
glances like cables
eye to eye.

The web
sways, sings like a trampoline

anchored in souls,
thump thump it goes
under the hobnails
of brute event.

And guts telling true
direction, dispersion
yield, out and out—
the whirling spool
(like the newborn
barely come from, and goodbye)—

You wouldn't dream
the leagues, the length
thousands, how generous—

but for the awakening,

the hand to hand,
'here, grasp
the lifeline,
(the Savior's
avalanche of
loaves and fishes

admixed like metaphor)'—

hope's rope.

BLIND

In a subway, epiphany
blazed before me;
PM crush, two young fellows
easy, companionable standing,
guitars slung back.

The train, blind as a worm,
lurched, inched
through Queens tunnel.

One, thrown off balance,
head snapped back,
turned toward me
eyes, milky white, dead agate.

Friends, the two, their
sightless, sunless moons.

And I wondered, conjured—
fingers of blind men,
deft as eyes, gentle, murmurous
summoning song alive.

Like Orpheus bereft
in a netherworld—
what to celebrate?

mysteries, eventualities
beyond, within
what we,
stuck in the obvious world,
name sight?

DWELLING

Gratutitous as a god
giving us dawn eastward—
(I know a few
godlike, plying
a like trade elsewhere)—

the cottage, arms outspread
like a mother, like Stringfellow's ghost,
the host; Come one, come all!

Around, scriptural waters
ebb and flow
no one pays for, not a farthing.

No fee, no false fealties, no
Low-life pennant lording over, only

the sky, fastened to centerpole
anchored to first day,
            proclaims
original blessing;
                    Be.

THE LOG

Easing a half-frozen log
into a fire half spent
like a cat's eye
spitting back,

I figure something of fate; yes
that's how
half I came, half shall go,
wanting, wondering—

and the best to come after—
residue, red, and alive.

AND YOU END WELL

Imagine, in December fury
the moon's eye
interlocuter, interloper, and
the sea swells
at Your coming—
familiar, a foundling
the sea knows the face of
beforehand,

and a hand
eases you out, here
where You
do and do not
landward, seaward
belong.

CREATION

Is the world to be thought
a greater scandal
to God
than to us?
I asked the babe in the manger.
I asked Herod.
I asked December that brought forth
mindless, this one and that.
And the tree
creaky in cold
queried
agreed
yes it might
under duress of law
bear a hundredweight
more or less
a lesser
to be borne
evil.

TO THE JESUITS

Like a First World Warrior
aloft
syncronizing
a ghost squadron—

he grins, raises powdery
fingers in V sign

such as dead pilots exchange
minutes after
the hell they lighted
darkens them.

Tell me, strike me dead
over & over & over
like the last barrel roll
of Richard Dix the ace

Who
who are the dead?

JOY

I.

I wish (it aches
to tell of it, ('aches,' yes—
the command, 'to tell of it')
Nevertheless, tell!
I wish for joy
so distant, how can I land on
that continent, from a sea
no map gives away?

I know the map,
I've never been there.

From afar, with what longing,
scanned it—all
wide smiles and wild surf.

O the ominous beard of winter,
benignity, the smile—Santa
packing a gun;
such malice

against maiden Spring
languishing
in an icy tower.

I don't know. If I knew
no need to wish.

'Do you know?'
(sings the maid in the tower)
'Yes?'
'how wrong, how wrong.'

II.

Joy overtook us. My brother home from prison.
The prose lies there on paper, papery
as lips of the dead. Unheeded.
Joy I've sought
O it was granted
beyond those words or these—one another.

My words were like eyes, redundant
closed eyes of the dead.
Not for nothing to see,
for everything. Closed against partial sight,
partial world, apportioned seas, approximations
(a bush afire, dew on a fleece, virgins, old women
heavy with hope's children.)

Who needs words?
partial, ourselves
in here, in now

a crossroad, lost, strangers seeking the way
from strangers; if lucky, honest strangers.

Their 'I'm not sure' the surest signpost
toward love's intersecting
darkness and truth.

A BUDDHIST CHANTS HIS EPITAPH

To have, to hold
is all the rage—
Turn a blank page
let go, let go.

THIS BOOK

As I walk patiently through life
poems follow close—
blind, dumb, agile, my own shadow,
the mind's dark overflow, the run of vein
we though red once, but know now, no.

Poem called death
is unwritten yet. Some day will show
the last line first
the shadow rise,
a bird of omen

snatch me for its ghost

and a hand somewhere,
purposeful as God's
close like two eyes, this book.